Guidelines and Games for Teaching Efficient Braille Reading

Guidelines and Games for Teaching Efficient Braille Reading

SECOND EDITION

Renae T. Bjorg, PhD
Myrna R. Olson, EdD

American Printing House for the Blind

Guidelines and Games for Teaching Efficient Braille Reading is copyright © 2022 by the American Printing House for the Blind. All rights reserved. This publication is protected by copyright and permission should be obtained from the publisher prior to any reproduction, storage in a retrieval system, or transmission in any form or by any means electronic, mechanical, photocopying, recording, or otherwise, unless where noted on specific pages. For information regarding permission, contact the publisher at APH Press, American Printing House for the Blind, 1839 Frankfort Ave, Louisville, KY 40206.

Library of Congress Cataloging-in-Publication Data

Names: Bjorg, Renae (Renae Therese), 1962- author. | Olson, Myrna R., author.
Title: Guidelines and games for teaching efficient braille reading / Renae T. Bjorg, Myrna R. Olson.
Description: Second edition. | Louisville, KY : APH Press, American printing house for the blind, [2022] | Includes bibliographical references and index. | Summary: "'Guidelines and Games for Teaching Efficient Braille Reading' is based on research in the areas of rapid reading and precision teaching, and offers unique guidelines and games ideas for adapting a general reading program to the needs of braille readers. This handbook serves as an invaluable resource to both supplement and enrich early braille instruction for classroom teachers and anyone working with children who are blind or visually impaired"-- Provided by publisher.
Identifiers: LCCN 2022011012 (print) | LCCN 2022011013 (ebook) | ISBN 9781950723102 (paperback) | ISBN 9781950723119 (epub)
Subjects: LCSH: Blind--Printing and writing systems. | Blind children--Education. | Educational games.
Classification: LCC HV1669 .B56 2022 (print) | LCC HV1669 (ebook) | DDC 686.2/82--dc23/eng/20220408
LC record available at https://lccn.loc.gov/2022011012
LC ebook record available at https://lccn.loc.gov/2022011013

Printed in the United States of America

www.aph.org

CONTENTS

Contributors	vi
Foreword	viii
In Memoriam	ix
Preface	xii
CHAPTER 1 **Introduction**	1
CHAPTER 2 **Background on Braille Reading**	6
CHAPTER 3 **Preschool Experiences Important to Emergent Braille Readers**	21
CHAPTER 4 **Activities for Teaching Braille More Efficiently at the Beginning Level**	34
CHAPTER 5 **Ideas for Working With Striving Readers**	57
CHAPTER 6 **Adding Spice to a Braille Reading Program with Activities and Games**	73
Appendices	
A – Nonfactual Questions for Checking Comprehension	99
B – Worksheet Ideas for Developing Braille Tactile Skills	101
Index	103

Authors

Renae Therese Bjorg, PhD, is an assistant professor in the Department of Teaching Leadership and Professional Practice at the University of North Dakota, where she is the program coordinator of the Visual Impairment specialization. Her research interests include the expanded core curriculum, especially independent living skills for students living in rural areas. She attended the University of North Dakota and taught at the North Dakota School for the Blind, Anne Carlsen Center for Children, and K–12 public schools. She also served children, ages birth to 3 years who were medically fragile and visually impaired, and their families. She currently lives with her husband in Grand Forks, North Dakota. They have a blended family of four adult children and seven grandchildren.

Myrna Raye Olson, EdD, was born and raised in North Dakota and attended North Dakota State University, Northern Montana College, Montana State University, San Francisco State University, and the University of North Dakota. She taught at the Montana School for the Deaf and Blind, the North Dakota School for the Blind, and the University of North Dakota. Her career at the University of North Dakota spanned 46 years; there, she developed and taught numerous courses in the fields of elementary, secondary, and special education, and served in various administrative positions. She retired in 2020 and lives in Grand Forks, North Dakota near her two sons, who are both teachers, and two grandsons.

Additional Contributors

Dave Beckett, EdD, consultant for the blind and visually impaired, Manitoba Department of Education, Manitoba Canada.

Sara R. Careless, MEd, consultant for the blind and visually impaired, Manitoba Department of Education in Manitoba, Canada.

Brittany D. Hagen, PhD, associate professor and accreditation coordinator, Division of Education, Mayville State University in Mayville, North Dakota.

Sandra R. Kenrick, MS, teacher of students with visual impairments, Rapid City, South Dakota.

Danielle Moelter-Swangstue, MS, teacher of students with visual impairments and special education strategist, Grand Forks, North Dakota.

Amy R. Neils, MS, teacher of students who are blind and visually impaired, South Central Service Cooperative, North Mankato, Minnesota.

Laura Roy, MS, coordinator of the Blind and Visually Impaired Services Unit, Manitoba Department of Education, Manitoba, Canada.

Austin T. Winger, PhD, instructional designer and adjunct faculty member for the University of North Dakota and the Grand Forks Public Schools, Grand Forks, North Dakota.

Foreword

It is an honor to write this foreword on the 40th anniversary of the first publication of *Guidelines and Games for Teaching Efficient Braille Reading* (1981).

Myrna Olson birthed this book because she was concerned about the low reading rates and poor mechanical habits demonstrated by her high-school students who were braille readers. In her quest to resolve this issue, she partnered with Sally Mangold, who had a long history of working with students who were visually impaired. Mangold was a braille reader, and her research focused on the development of good mechanical skills during beginning braille instruction. These pioneers set the standards for excellence in teaching foundational skills to beginning braille readers, enabling students to develop and maintain good reading habits and achieve high levels of reading without sacrificing comprehension levels. The book they wrote, based on their research, continues to be a top seller and integral to the field.

While this version of *Guidelines and Games for Teaching Efficient Braille Reading* has been updated to reflect current research and language (e.g., use of braille displays and other assistive technology was at the infancy stage in previous editions), the heart of the book and the structure of it remains intact. It is anticipated that this book will educate and inspire leaders to reach the levels of excellence established by the original authors.

Renae Bjorg, PhD
Assistant Professor
University of North Dakota

In Memoriam

The quality of life need not be compromised because of a visual impairment. Love, tenderness, pride in one's accomplishments are never measured in terms of physical characteristics.

—Sally Mangold

Sally Mangold teaching a braille class

I first met Sally Mangold in the summer of 1976 when I traveled with five students of mine from the University of North Dakota to San Francisco State University to obtain advanced coursework in blindness and visual impairment. Sally was brilliant, competent, and friendly. She, Philip Hatlen, and Pete Wurzberger taught me much about blindness and visual impairment that summer. My students and I were mesmerized by their expertise, teaching strategies, and warm personalities.

Sally was an extremely positive person who made an enormous impact on everyone fortunate enough to meet her. She was small in stature but a giant in terms of her expertise. She won many awards and was one of the first teachers of students with visual impairments in public schools. Sally and her husband, who was also visually impaired, co-founded the company Educational Technology Aids. She had an enormous impact on the way I subsequently taught braille and deserves credit for the book I initially wrote and the one Renae Bjorg and I have revised.

Sally taught students with visual impairments ranging from kindergarten through high school for 18 years. After receiving her PhD from the University of California, Berkley in 1977, she served as a professor at San Francisco State University from 1977 to 1995. She published over 45 books, articles, and videos as of 2004.

One of the awards that Sally won was the Migel Medal from the American Foundation for the Blind. As Hatlen noted, she was one of the most successful and inspirational teachers in the Castro Valley Schools in California. Visitors from all over the world came to visit the programs that Sally developed in these schools. Particularly noteworthy was Sally's practice of asking parents what they wanted their child to learn.

Other awards received by Mangold include the Association for Education and Rehabilitation of the Blind and Visually Impaired's Josephine L. Taylor Leadership Award in 1996, California Transcribers and Educators for the Blind and Visually Impaired's Fred Sinclair Award in 2000, and the Holbrook-Humphries Literacy Award in 2001.

Myrna Olson, EdD
Professor
University of North Dakota
Retired 2020 (46 years of service)

Sally Mangold has had a profound impact on me personally and professionally; she shaped who I am as a teacher.

Thirty years ago, I sat in Sally's class at San Francisco State University. During the introduction to the course, she said, "Don't bother raising your hand. It won't do any good." For a minute, I wondered how I was going to get her attention, but I soon discovered that she was one of the most personable women I would ever meet. She could be speaking in a crowded room and leave everyone feeling as if they were sitting one-on-one with her at her kitchen table chatting over a warm cup of coffee. She was brilliant and had a way of making everyone around her feel at ease. Even in situations where she was ridiculed or demeaned in public because of her blindness, she was gracious and took time to educate the waiter, the couple in the next booth in a restaurant, or the person at the Bay Area Rapid Transit (BART). It was inspiring to watch how she eased the fears and debunked the myths people had about disabilities. She never chastised; instead, she empowered people to ask questions and embrace humanity.

While there are many ways that Sally impacted me, there was one defining moment that shaped who I am as a teacher. Sally and her husband Phil owned a very successful business and operated it from their garage. During a tour, Phil showed my husband and me how he took calls and documented orders using his slate and stylus. There were numerous aisles of equipment, and everything was totally organized and labeled in braille. It was in that moment that braille became real to me. It had a central purpose and function. No longer a code, braille was a key for my students to unlock doors to creativity, self-expression, and independence.

I am deeply grateful for Sally Mangold. She loved life and did not let blindness get in the way of living it to the fullest. I often think about how her fingers, adorned in red nail polish, danced across the braille pages as she read notes for an audience or personal pleasure. Her legacy of a life well lived continues on through my students.

Julie Anderson, MS
Teacher of Students with Visual Impairments K–12
Fargo Public Schools, Fargo, ND
Adjunct Professor
University of North Dakota

Preface

Braille has been upheld as a worthwhile mode of reading for individuals who are blind or have a visual impairment since its invention. It affords the reader several advantages over auditory reading modes—a form of independence, a means of notetaking, a way of learning spelling and punctuation, and an opportunity to review material that has been read previously. Its bulkiness and high cost are definite drawbacks, but the overriding disadvantage of braille is the length of time consumed in tactually reading it. The average speed of braille readers falls progressively behind the average speed of print readers as braille readers move through the grades. Consequently, adult braille readers often read much more slowly than sighted adults.

Most of my five years as a teacher of students with visual impairments in the residential school setting was spent working with children who had already been taught to read braille. I was frustrated by the rate at which my students read as well as by their various bad mechanical habits. In 1974, I began training teachers in the area of visual impairment at the University of North Dakota. Conducting research for my dissertation at the time, I became interested in the writings of Vearl McBride of Culver-Stockton College in Canton, Missouri. An article appearing in the *New Outlook for the Blind* reported reading rate gains over 400 percent for braille readers after a two-week workshop conducted by McBride. Comprehension levels for these readers were said to have dropped slightly, but no standardized test was given to measure the amount.

In August 1974, I received permission to administer a standardized test to the braille reading participants in one of McBride's workshops. The reading rate gains on this test were much more modest (30–35 percent) than those recorded through informal testing (≥ 200 percent). Comprehension levels did, however, remain stable at a satisfactory level (≥ 80 percent). Following that workshop, I taught a workshop of my own based upon McBride's procedures and obtained results that were not significantly different from McBride's. One of the more interesting conclusions of my research was the negative correlation I found between age and percent increase in reading rate achieved by participants in both workshops. It seemed that the longer one had been entrenched in bad reading habits, the more difficult it was to break those habits. During an informal follow-up, I also discovered that few workshop participants maintained their gains in reading rate.

It became clear to me that rather than attempt "remedial" instruction with adult readers, it would be better to teach braille incorporating rapid reading principles beginning with the readiness level of reading. I considered writing a book at the time but felt a need for information and feedback from someone who had taught more beginning braille reading than I had. This need was met during the summer of 1977, when I met Sally Mangold at a summer session at San Francisco State University. She had been a resource teacher of students who were blind or visually impaired for 15 years and had recently completed her doctoral study on the topic of braille reading. She had discovered there was an advantage to concentrating on the development of good mechanical skills during beginning braille instruction.

Over the years, Sally and I managed to collaborate on the first edition of this book by means of long-distance phone calls and while attending the same conventions across the country. Sally's background in reading-related research and experience as a resource teacher, coupled with the fact that she was a braille user, made her contributions to the first five chapters extremely valuable. In addition, she wrote Chapter 6 on games and activities to add "spice" to a braille reading program. This book offers something unique. It provides parents, teachers of students with visual impairments, and general education teachers with ideas for adapting a general reading program to the needs of braille readers. Activities and games offered provide enrichment to the traditional teaching of braille reading skills from the preschool level through Grade 3. Suggestions for working with remedial readers, regardless of age, are also provided.

Myrna R. Olson, EdD

CHAPTER 1

Introduction

Audience and Intent

This book on braille reading is intended for parents, preschool educators, resource and itinerant teachers, and teachers of students with visual impairments. Many of the ideas presented will also be helpful to teachers who work with braille readers in the general education setting.

Anyone teaching a child to read braille should have a knowledge of the braille code and an understanding of the major reading methods.

Knowledge of the Braille Code

Any individual planning to introduce braille to another person must have adequate knowledge of the braille reading code in order to decide a sequence for the introduction of contractions and analyze the student's reading errors.

If a formal course on braille is unavailable in the local community, the following self-instructional materials can be utilized:

1. The National Library Service for the Blind and Print Disabled, Library of Congress, offers a free course to teach students to transcribe print materials into braille (loc.gov/nls/about/services/braille-transcription-proofreading-courses/). Upon successful course completion, students receive a certificate in literary braille transcribing. A manual braillewriter, a computer with a six-key direct input software program, or a 40-cell slate is required to produce the braille.

2. *Ashcroft's Programmed Instruction: Unified English Braille* consists of 12 chapters (scalarspublishing.com). Students learn the braille code in a systematic way. Answer keys to the practice lessons are provided so students are able to receive immediate feedback. The *Companion Reader* is produced in braille and can be used for supplementary reading. A manual braillewriter or a computer with a six-key direct input software program is required to complete this course.

3. *Braille Brain: A Braille Training Program for Educators and Family Members* (Kim Blackwell, Cheryl Kamei-Hannan, & Gina Michell, 2021) is a training program funded by the US Department of Education, Rehabilitation Services Agency, (H235E190002). The overall goal of the project is to promote literacy and STEM instruction provided by pre-service and in-service teachers of students with visual impairments, paraprofessionals, parents, and educational team members.

    The Braille Brain microsite (pathstoliteracy.org/braille-brain) consists of three main components: (a) braille training materials that focus on UEB literary braille and Nemeth Braille, (b) braille reading and writing assessment, and (c) instructional materials and evidence-based practices that support braille literacy and STEM instruction.

4. The Canadian National Institute for the Blind (CNIB) offers a Unified English Braille Transcription Course that is geared toward transcribers, proofreaders, and teachers of braille reading (cnib.ca/en/unified-english-braille-ueb-transcription-course?region=on).

5. Hadley offers courses to learn the braille code visually through a series of interactive online workshops or tactually through audio-delivered courses (hadley.edu/learn?topic_id=15).

6. *Unified English Braille Australian Training Manual* (2016) is a series of lessons and practice exercises for teachers, transcribers, and parents to learn braille.

7. *UEB Online* (uebonline.org/) offers online training programs in braille literacy and is free to anyone who wants to learn braille. A computer and Internet connection are required.

Whichever self-directed text or program a person chooses, access to a braille writing device will be necessary. Many state schools for the blind will loan a braillewriter to individuals who want to learn braille. At approximately $800, the cost of buying a braillewriter may be prohibitive.

The slate and stylus (equivalent to a paper and pencil) are inexpensive, starting at less than $20 and are made of a variety of materials such as metal or plastic. The Janus Interline Braille Slate with Saddle-Shaped Stylus is plastic and allows for 11 lines of writing. The user is able to write on both sides of a standard 3-by-5-inch index card without having to remove the card. It is enclosed on three sides, and one of the 3-inch sides is open and notched for easy insertion of the index card. The cost of this tool is $5.

In the past, many individuals who are blind were taught to write braille with a slate and stylus from the beginning; current trends in teaching postpone its introduction as a writing tool until the braille code has been mastered. While some people argue that the slate and stylus are obsolete, it is important that students who are blind or visually impaired have the option to choose the right tool for the task. Learning to use the slate and stylus efficiently provides more choices.

Understanding of the Major Reading Methods

The methods used to teach reading are as varied as the abilities of young children learning to read. However, it is imperative that teachers of braille are familiar with the essential elements of evidence-based literacy instruction. This knowledge leads to application of best practices. The following paragraphs provide an overview of the essential elements to include in an evidence-based approach to teaching reading.

Recent rhetoric surrounding best practices for reading instruction has focused on the science of reading. The science of reading is not necessarily a program of reading instruction or a specific reading strategy, but rather a collective consensus on the scientific research related to how students learn to read and what types of reading instruction benefits readers most. The science of reading is based on scientific research conducted in various fields including neuroscience, cognitive psychology, pedagogical practices, and linguistics. The empirical research provides insights on how children learn to read, which skills are necessary for reading, and how the brain develops in young readers (Ordetx, 2021).

Burkins and Yates (2021), accomplished reading practitioners, discuss the importance of teachers appraising current practices of teaching reading and how those align with evidence-based practices. These practices include teaching foundational reading skills, such as phonics and comprehension, in explicit and direct ways. These methods have been shown to improve students' reading achievement and confirm that there is one correct way to teach reading—through research-based practices known as the science of reading.

Furthermore, teachers of reading should incorporate explicit instructional and assessment practices framed around the National Reading Panel's (2000) five components of reading: phonemic awareness, phonics, fluency, vocabulary, and comprehension. *Phonemic awareness* is a reader's ability to identify and manipulate individual sounds, called phonemes in spoken words. Because it is a predictor of early reading success, phonemic awareness is an essential element to include in an evidence-based reading instruction approach and requires explicit teaching (Kilpatrick, 2015) to braille and non-braille readers.

A second element of reading instruction requiring explicit teaching is phonics instruction. While phonemic awareness relates to the spoken sounds, phonics instruction focuses on the connection between spoken sounds and written letters. When students learn that letters make sounds and sounds combine to make words, they can apply this knowledge to decode familiar and new words, building their reading fluency.

Reading fluency relates to a reader's ability to read words with accuracy, speed, and expression. *Fluency* occurs when readers can recognize words quickly and say them aloud with expression. Readers who are not fluent struggle to read words accurately, quickly, or with appropriate expression. Readers who have strong fluency do not need to focus on decoding words and can concentrate their efforts on comprehending what the words mean.

Another essential element of evidence-based reading instruction is vocabulary instruction. *Vocabulary* refers to the variety of words readers need to know and understand. Explicit vocabulary instruction helps students better comprehend what they are reading. Duke and Cartwright (2021) suggest that knowledge of vocabulary terms affects reading comprehension and word recognition. Teachers of braille should use explicit vocabulary instruction to introduce students to new concepts and ideas.

Comprehension, some would argue, is the ultimate objective of reading. One reads to understand and interpret what they have read. Comprehending text happens when readers can decode words quickly and accurately and identify the meaning of vocabulary within the text. Because teaching explicit comprehension strategies predicts students' ability to read successfully, it is important for teachers to include strategies in their instruction that align with the science of reading (Duke & Cartwright, 2021).

In conclusion, advances in research related to reading instruction show that the essential elements of teaching reading overlap in several ways, and it is critical for teachers of reading to be abreast of the most recent and relevant research. Being equipped with research-based practices helps teachers apply learned methods to braille readers.

Organization and Content of the Book

The remainder of this chapter is devoted to a synopsis of this book by individual chapter.

Chapter 2: Background on Braille Reading

The history of braille reading is interpreted broadly to include a discussion of its development, nature, and use. The advantages of braille over other non-print reading modes are discussed, followed by a summary of the basic perceptual nature of braille reading as compared to print reading. The latter portion of this chapter is devoted to a review of the literature relating to the braille reading habits of children and the common approaches to teaching braille.

Chapter 3: Preschool Experiences Important to Emergent Braille Readers

Specific suggestions are offered to parents, teachers, and preschool workers for providing pertinent pre-braille experiences to young children. The unique needs of children who are blind are addressed within the framework of sensory-motor development, concept development, and reading awareness.

Chapter 4: Activities for Teaching Braille More Efficiently at the Beginning Level

In this chapter, numerous activities are suggested to use with braille readers in the skill areas listed below. Most of the activities are geared to make braille reading a more efficient process.

1. Attitude Development
2. Mechanical Skills and Ergonomics
3. Hand Movements and Finger Positions
4. Light Finger Touch
5. Tactile Perception and Discrimination
6. Comprehension Skills
7. Flexibility Skills

8. Reading Style Development

9. Memorization of the Braille Code Rules

Suggested in the final section of this chapter are various ways of facilitating carry-over of braille skills learned in a special setting to the general education classroom.

Chapter 5: Ideas for Working With Striving Readers
Specific suggestions for working with various types of "striving readers" are given. The first part of the chapter identifies difficulties of the striving reader in general. Prescriptions are given for working on problems falling into 14 different skill areas. The latter portion of the chapter is devoted to special considerations that must be given to striving readers who are former print readers.

Chapter 6: Adding Spice to a Braille Reading Program with Activities and Games
The activities and games outlined in this chapter are appropriate for readers from level pre-K through Grade 3, regardless of their chronological ages. Some activities can be used with older students who have experienced a recent vision loss. The hope is that these activities will help students maintain high motivation toward learning to read, while reinforcing the skills that have been introduced.

References

Burkins, J., & Yates, K. (2021). *Shifting the balance: 6 ways to bring the science of reading into the balanced literacy classroom.* Stenhouse Publishers.

Duke, N., & Cartwright, K. (2021). The science of reading progresses: Communicating advances beyond the simple view of reading. *Reading Research Quarterly, 56*(51), S25–S44. https://doi.org/10.1002/rrq.411

Eunice Kennedy Shriver National Instittue of Chld Health and Human Development, NIH, DHHS. (2000). *Report of the National Reading Panel: Teaching Children to Read: Report of the Subgroups.* https://nichd.nih.gov/sites/default/files/publications/pubs/nrp/Documents/report.pdf

Holbrook, M. Cay, D'Andrea, M., (2014). *Ashcroft's Programmed Instruction: Unified English Braille. (4th ed.).* Scalars Publishing.

Holbrook, M. Cay & D'Andrea, M. (2014). *Ashcroft's Programmed Instruction Companion Reader: Unified English Braille.* Scalars Publishing.

Kilpatrick, D. A. (2015). *Essentials of assessing, preventing, and overcoming reading difficulties.* John Wiley & Sons, Inc.

Ordetx, K. (2021). What is the science of reading? *Institute for Multi-Sensory Education (IMSE) Journal.* https://journal.imse.com/what-is-the-science-of-reading/

CHAPTER 2

Background on Braille Reading

Braille is the key to literacy and it is literacy that opens the doors to opportunities for independence.

—Sally Mangold

Development of a Standardized Braille Code

The tactile system of reading known as braille came to be over a long period of time. In the 1700s, Valentin Haüy first introduced the concept of embossed print letters, which had little success. This led the way for the development of the tactually perceptible code in the early 19th century by Charles Barbier, a French army officer. His code enabled his men to send and receive messages at night. Louis Braille learned Barbier's system but found it had serious drawbacks. Still only 15 years old, Braille decided to create his own method, and by 1824 had come up with a reading system using embossed dots. The official adoption of his new system by the Royal Institution for Blind Youth, where Braille was a student, did not happen until much later. In 1869, the Missouri School for the Blind became the first institution in the United States to adopt the code.

For decades, the advantages and disadvantages of the new system were argued by educators of students with visual impairments. Not until 1932 did the United States finally reach an agreement with England to accept English braille (contracted) as a standard form for embossing. The Joint Uniform Braille Committee (JUBC) modified the 1932 code in 1959. To keep the literary code concurrent with innovations and formats being used in print, further minor revisions were made in 1962, 1966, and 1968. Braille Authority of North America (BANA) was established in 1977 and continued to revise the braille code to reflect current practice.

In the early 1990s, work began on a major revision to the English American Edition braille code with the intent to establish a code that would unify literary, mathematics, and computing braille symbols and be applied to English language material across multiple countries.

After considerable input from international stakeholders, including braille readers, educators, and transcribers, the Unified English Braille Code (UEB) was established. The revised code was based on the literary braille code while incorporating mathematical and technical symbols and rules so that it could be used across literary and technical contexts. It is a code designed to be more flexible with less restrictive rules for the use of contractions (Risjord, 2014).

In April 2004, the International Council on English Braille (ICEB) General Assembly approved the unification of different braille codes into the UEB and recognized it as the international standard for English braille. In November 2012, BANA adopted the UEB as the official code in the United States for all transcriptions including technical materials. As of 2016, the official codes in the United States are UEB, the Nemeth Braille Code for Mathematics and Science Notation, the Music Braille Code, and the International Phonetic Alphabet Braille Code. Other countries, such as Canada, have adopted UEB as the official code for literary, mathematical, and technical transcription.

The UEB code consists of alphabet letters, numbers, punctuation, indicators, contractions, and math symbols. The braille cell consists, as always, of two vertical rows of three dots each, shown below.

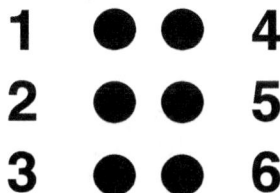

Many investigators have concerned themselves with establishing optimal dot size, dot configuration, and spacing among the dots. The official spacing used today was reported to be mutually beneficial for children and adults. It provides 0.09 inch between dot centers, both vertically and horizontally within a cell. Between cells, the spacing is 0.16 inch and the dot height is 0.025 inch, or somewhat less. This sizing continues to be the standard size for braille production today.

Nature of Tactual Reading

Millar (1987) conducted a study to test hand functions and how they are used by fast readers in two-handed reading. Specifically, Millar sought to test the hypothesis that "two reading fingers touch letters simultaneously and that this occurs more frequently than any other type of finger position" (p. 112).

An apparatus to record the reader's voice and timing synchronously was used to study finger positions of both hands during braille reading. Ten high school students, considered to be fluent braillists, were selected to participate in the study. Each participant was asked to read an assigned story after reading at least two warm-up stories.

Millar found the results to be "surprising" (1987, p. 114) because they were opposite of the hypothesis that fluent readers used both hands to read simultaneously. Of the six different simultaneous finger positions that were identified, simultaneous touching of letters by the two hands occurred the least often while touching a letter and a space occurred most frequently. These findings suggest that two fingers function differently when moving synchronously and readers "were mainly sampling dot-gap patterns rather than discreet letter shapes" (p. 119). Millar concluded that "fluency does not depend on simultaneous processing of the same type of information, but on fast intermittent alternation in function between the two hands" (1987, p. 121).

Kusajima (1974) conducted an experimental investigation of the physiology and psychology of visual and tactual reading. The comparisons that he drew between the two modes from his investigation are summarized below.

Pause and Movement

In visual reading, the eye moves in a series of rapid jumps, alternately pausing briefly and then moving again. In this way, fixation on points along a line of text is combined with jumping eye movements. During long pauses, letters, words, or short sentences are perceived all at once; no recognition occurs during jumping movements. Most reading time is spent in pauses (92–98 percent). In contrast, during braille reading, pauses are rare. When the finger stops moving, only the letter under the finger is read. Thus, the fingers read braille through movement.

Number and Location of Pauses

When visual reading skills improve, the number of pauses declines and becomes more rhythmic. In braille reading, fewer up-and-down, zig-zag movements, and irregular finger pressures indicate increasing skill. For both modes of reading, any means of reducing wasted motion is desirable. The location of pauses in visual and braille reading is not related to meaning, grammar, or rhetoric.

Function of Pauses and Movements

In visual reading, letters, words, or short sentences are perceived all at once during pauses, but in braille reading, characters are perceived successively. Thus, the unit of perception is much wider in visual reading than it is in tactual reading. Nevertheless, on the basis of the number of perceptual units covered in braille, it is not as slow as one would predict. This is best explained by regarding the reading process as perception combined with other factors.

Methods of Perception

The best visual readers apprehend sentences through groups of words or even short sentences. For braille readers, Kusajima concludes that letters are perceived successively through movement of the fingers. The best braille readers, then, group letters in perception. Nolan and Kederis (1969) found the basic perceptual unit in braille reading to be the individual braille cell. The fact that most teachers successfully use a whole-word method in teaching braille suggests that further research is needed in this area.

Crandell (1974) suggested that two kinds of perceptual windows are employed by a braille reader—one spatial (the braille cell) and the other temporal. Even though each spatial unit must be recognized sequentially, he proposed that a relatively large number of these units are processed in a given time period. Information received through the senses is then accumulated and sequenced into temporal units and processed as a single unit. The more spatial units accommodated in the temporal units, the more total information available to the perceiver. The length of the temporal unit may vary from less than a second to several seconds.

Dominant and Subordinate Characters

In visual reading, word recognition depends on context and shape characteristics; letter shapes may be dominant or subordinate in characterizing the form of a word. The situation is similar in braille reading. The average braille reader obtains clues from the first one, two, or three characters in a word; these become the dominant letters in the sentence.

Good and Poor Reading

Good or poor reading is determined by a combination of the reader's ability, experiences, and mechanical habits, as well as the difficulty of the material being read. Good visual reading is characterized by a small number of short regular pauses, no regressive movements, well-adjusted return sweeps, and an accurate understanding of the text. Good braille reading is characterized by few zig-zag, up-and-down, or fluttering movements, uniform pressure on the fingertips, no regressive movements, coordinated movements between lines with both hands, and accurate textual understanding.

Return Sweeps and Movements Between Lines

Visual return sweeps are generally shorter than the line of text, since the pauses at the beginning and end of the sentence are usually within the line. In one-handed braille reading, return sweep length between successive lines of text are longer than the text line because tactual verification of the line's beginning and end is necessary. For both types of reading, the eye or finger movements become habituated motor acts. In bimanual (two-handed) braille reading, the trailing finger helps control the movement of the leading (or reading) finger, preventing over- or underestimated return sweep movements. While the reading finger finishes one line of text, the trailing finger returns to the location of the beginning of the next line and awaits contact with the reading finger. The reading finger moves quickly to make this contact, and then both read along to the middle of the line. At this point, the trailing finger separates to make the return sweep.

Both Eyes and Both Hands

Since the mechanical movement of the eyes in the same direction is involuntary, independent movement of the eyes across different lines of print is physiologically impossible. In contrast, both hands are under voluntary control during braille reading. The accompaniment of the trailing finger widens the perceptual aperture. Reassurance is attained by reading with both hands. A bimanual reader can "hold" at the place where a point is missed and return their reading finger to that spot for review. Misprints, spoiled embossed dots, obscure characters, and difficult or unfamiliar words can be indexed by the trailing finger while the reading finger scans to help organize meaning. Additionally, fingers on both hands can be used for reading, with fingers on either hand serving as the indexers and those of the other hand searchers of meaning through context.

Studies on Braille Reading Habits of Children

There have been several studies of braille reading habits, and the three most comprehensive will be summarized here.

Maxfield (1928) found that two-handed braille readers are superior readers. In addition, right-handed braille readers are more efficient readers than left-handed readers. She observed the best readers read ahead with the left hand before finishing the preceding line with the right hand. Further suggestions made by Maxfield as a result of her study were:

1. The fingertips should not be pressed down too heavily.
2. Children should be taught to read with both hands.
3. Excessive up-and-down motion of the fingertips should be discouraged.
4. Books should be held parallel with the edge of the table or at a narrow, acute angle.
5. Lip movement and inner speech should be discouraged since they retard reading speed.

Biirklen (1932) tested 66 readers and found that one-fourth of them had no hand preference for reading braille; three-fourths of this group read slightly better with the left hand than with the right hand, which is inconsistent with Maxfield's findings. Biirklen further found that the index fingers of both hands were used most frequently and best for reading, with the middle fingers used secondarily, and other fingers less frequently. Touch movements of good readers proceeded in a straight line while those of poor readers were serrated and twisted. As in Maxfield's study, pressure of the fingertips was more slight and uniform among good readers as compared to poor readers. He observed that touch sensitivity decreased only a small amount after several hours of braille reading. General fatigue was also found to be negligible after extended braille reading. Biirklen's subjects read, on the average, three to four times slower than sighted print individuals; however, he used uncontracted braille in his study. In uncontracted braille, every letter of each word is brailled. Contracted braille is a form of shorthand where some words have shortcuts (e.g., the letter "l" represents the word like or "fr" represents friend). Reading with both hands was found to be the most efficient among his subjects; single-handed braille readers' reading time was nearly double that of two-handed braille readers. Biirklen concluded that arm and body positions were important to efficient braille reading as well. Along these lines, he suggested that book height be such that arm and hand movements were unhampered. He recognized that in braille, the most used letters were not identical with the most readable ones.

Several changes occurred in the teaching of braille reading after the Maxfield and Biirklen studies. Contracted braille began to be introduced from the beginning of reading instruction. Braille printing underwent changes, which made braille books more available and less expensive. Methods of teaching braille also changed.

Lowenfeld, Abel, and Hatlen (1969) conducted a study in an attempt to assess the effects of some of these changes. Two hundred blind students attending public or residential schools were participants. Half of the students were fourth graders and half were eighth graders. An analysis of the reading behavior of these students showed:

1. There was no significant difference in reading comprehension and rate scores among students using the left hand, the right hand, or both hands.
2. Eighth graders who found the next line with their left hand and read ahead with it while the right hand finished the preceding line were more efficient readers than their peers who did not use this method.
3. Superior braille readers tended to read in an even flow and did not rub letters, lose their place when reading, or accompany their reading with silent speech movements.
4. Students who read without mannerisms and were more relaxed while reading were superior readers.
5. Posture during reading appeared to have no influence on reading efficiency.
6. "Avid" braille readers were superior readers.

The Alphabetic Braille and Contracted Braille Study (ABC Braille Study) investigated whether the approach to teaching braille contractions affected reading rates in young children (Wall Emerson et al., 2009). Participants from Canada and the United States were divided into two groups. One group initially learned to read and write using uncontracted braille, while the other group used fully contracted braille from the beginning. Wall Emerson et al. reported that reading rates did not significantly correlate to the number of contractions a student was exposed to or taught. They found that both groups had lower reading rates when compared to the norms of print readers. Students in this study did not receive any specific reading speed training or intervention like the methods described above. Researchers acknowledge that this may have affected the overall reading rates.

Current State of Braille

Braille reading and writing remains one of the primary means of communication for individuals who have a significant visual impairment. However, advances in technology have provided alternative ways to read, write, store, and produce braille.

With the use of screen-reading software and refreshable braille displays, individuals who are visually impaired can access print information readily using a computer, tablet, or smartphone. Today, paper braille is no longer the only way a person who is visually impaired can write and read. Individuals who are visually impaired will often use a word-processing program to type information into a document, or they may dictate using speech-to-text software.

Additionally, individuals can read braille electronically with the aid of a refreshable braille display wirelessly connected to a device of their choice.

Despite these advances in technology, certain information—such as complex mathematical and scientific notation or tables and diagrams—is best read in braille. As Mellor (1979) previously found, the use of braille is unsurpassed by other mediums for: (a) reading tables and diagrams; (b) reading technical or difficult material; (c) demanding the reader to be an active participant rather than a passive listener; (d) providing individuals who are blind their sole means of reading.

Innovations in Braille Reading, Writing and Production
Braille Without Paper

Innovations in braille technology have changed the way individuals with visual impairments learn the braille code. Although the classic, manual Perkins Brailler remains the tool of choice by many educators for teaching students the braille code and the mechanics of writing braille, there are alternative electronic options such as the Perkins SMART Brailler and the Mountbatten Brailler. Both of these machines incorporate modern technology to allow for a lighter touch and provide audio feedback, resulting in increased motivation for students learning the braille code (Michaelson et al., 2015). Braille technology is now an essential component of a braille literacy program for students who are blind.

In addition to newer electric braillers, advances in technology have resulted in numerous electronic devices that provide the option to read braille in a digital format on a refreshable braille display. These paperless devices have electronic pins that are raised or lowered in different combinations to represent braille characters. A refreshable braille display is connected with a cable or wirelessly via Bluetooth, to a computer, portable tablet, or smartphone, and when paired with screen-reading software, will translate information displayed on the screen into readable text on the braille display. Refreshable braille devices now range in size from 14 to 80 braille cells in length.

Another paperless option is the electronic braille notetaker, which can be used independently of a computer or portable device. These all-in-one devices are equipped with a braille or standard keyboard, a refreshable braille display, and a built-in speech synthesizer. They typically incorporate word processors, calendars, calculators, or clocks, and have web-browsing capabilities that function similar to a standard computer.

The advantages of refreshable braille machines are numerous. There is a tremendous reduction in the storage space needed for braille materials; students can conveniently carry their compact notetaking device or braille display with their braille books stored digitally to and from school. The information-handling features of these devices provide students with flexibility in writing assignments, allowing them to edit and correct mistakes and file notes in a digital file folder system on their computer or notetaker.

The use of refreshable braille displays or notetaking devices has become more widespread. It is now common for most students who are blind and using braille to be introduced to a refreshable braille device and a computer or a notetaker early in their education as part of the technology component of the expanded core curriculum. With keys that are easy to press and refreshable braille pins providing reliably crisp dots, electronic braille notetakers may provide added motivation for learning braille (Bickford & Falco, 2012).

This alternative to the traditional method of producing and accessing hard-copy braille means increased access to print documents, books, and information available on the Internet. Nonetheless, resources must be in a file format accessible to the user, and not all web pages are created to be accessible with a screen-reading software program.

These advances in technology have made braille more accessible in a digital format. Individuals who prefer to read braille no longer have to wait for a current title to be transcribed, embossed, and shipped, but can now access online accessible files as they become available and read them using a device connected to a braille display. The availability of digital files increases access to print; however, the simultaneous release of accessible files or electronic braille files with print titles—which would make distribution even more inclusive—remains an elusive goal.

Although accessible technology continues to be expensive (e.g., up to $10,000 for an 80-cell refreshable braille display), the cost of refreshable braille devices is slowly falling, rendering them more accessible and ultimately providing greater access to print materials without the wait time for transcription.

Braille Production

Braille translation software takes digital print text and translates it into braille text. The most widely used braille translation software worldwide is the Duxbury Braille Translator (DBT). Established in 1975, DBT supports over 170 languages in uncontracted or contracted literary, mathematical or technical braille, including UEB. More recently, the American Printing House for the Blind (APH) developed a new choice in braille translation software, Braille Blaster, which relies on Liblouis, an open-source braille translator.

Braille translation software combines word-processing capabilities with braille transcription and allows individuals to work in either print or braille. Print documents can be imported into the software for quick translation into braille; however, the expertise of a certified braille transcriber and proofreader is necessary to ensure all formatting rules are applied and braille contractions are correct. A high level of expertise is required to transcribe mathematical and technical material.

Computer generated braille can be printed on a braille embosser with relative ease. Industrial embossers are used by production centers across the world and can emboss either single-sided or double-sided (interpoint) pages, some at a speed of 1,000–1,300 pages per hour. They can produce six- or eight-dot braille, and some embossers also have the capability of embossing tactile graphics.

Desktop embossers for home, school, or office applications are increasingly popular and provide the option of printing from computers, braille notetakers, mobile devices, or a flash drive. These embossers often include the single- or double-sided printing feature, providing options for the quick translation and embossing of materials as needed.

Alternatives to Braille

Although there is not a medium that can completely replace the tactile experience of reading braille, sophisticated speech synthesizer software—in combination with accessible file formats—is now available and can be used to supplement braille.

Reading by listening is an obvious way to gain access to print and can be more efficient than braille because of the interaction between speed and comprehension. For example, Nolan (1966) found information absorbed by listening required approximately one-third of the time necessary for tactual reading, and, furthermore, comprehension remained stable. Compressed speech devices have permitted listening at a rate of 275 words per minute without loss of comprehension (Orr et al., 1965). Braille reading is much slower, as reading rates for high school students have been reported at 110 words per minute (Lowenfeld et al., 1969).

Attempts to develop machines that can optically scan printed material and produce intelligible sounds date back to 1919, when the optophone was demonstrated in England. The machine scanned a printed page and produced coded sounds corresponding to printed letters (Jameson, 1966). Few people ever learned to use the machine because it proved difficult to learn the sound code and reading speeds were slow (Hanninen, 1975). With advances in technology, Optical Character Recognition (OCR) software has become sophisticated and relatively easy to use. Hard-copy print documents can be scanned using a traditional flatbed scanner and OCR software, allowing individuals to read print materials that would otherwise be inaccessible. Additionally, there are an increasing number of OCR applications, which can be downloaded for use on a tablet or smartphone that provide solutions for quick scanning and access to print. In combination with a smartphone, OCR software allows individuals with visual impairments to read incidental print found in the community, such as signage, package labeling, and pricing, as well as restaurant menus that formerly were inaccessible.

Technology advances continue at a rapid speed, and improvements provide individuals with visual impairments ready access to print information, increasing their independence. Sophisticated speech synthesizers offer excellent quality of sound and access to information at a high speed, providing a means of reading through listening superior to braille in terms of efficiency. Screen-reading software and OCR provide immediate access to information that conventional braille production techniques cannot. These are useful alternatives to braille, and individuals who are visually impaired need to be taught the skills necessary to navigate the plethora of access technology now available.

Despite the increased access to electronic files and print information through speech synthesizers, the ability to read braille remains a priority in the development of literacy skills for those who are visually impaired. Although they complement braille, screen readers and other assistive reading technologies are not as effective as braille in developing literacy for individuals who are blind.

Even with all of the new technology, the continual development of greater efficiency in one's ability to read braille and the skills needed to be fluent across technology and electronic file platforms should be prioritized. The use of electronic braille files with a refreshable braille device increases the access to and the portability of braille, assuming the reader has the required braille literacy skills to read the information presented in this manner.

Attempts to Increase Braille Reading Rates

Braille readers, on average, read at a slower rate (words per minute) than print readers (Foulke, 1979, Trent & Truan, 1997). While this is expected due to the nature of braille reading, an individual's reading speed remains an important part of reading fluency, which in turn contributes to overall braille literacy (Stanfa & Johnson, 2015). The benefits of braille literacy are many, including higher levels of independence, confidence, and self-esteem.

Over the years, researchers have trialed a variety of training methods and devices in search of finding a way to increase braille reading rates. Grunwald (1966), Heber (1967), and Kederis (1971) experimented with mechanical devices (e.g., tachistoscope) designed to move braille continuously. Typically, these devices moved braille from right to left across an exposed presentation window. Results from these studies were mixed. While Heber found three of these devices were successful in improving braille reading rates of children and adults, Kederis found no significant increase when using two such machines. Advances in technology later allowed Cates and Sowell (1990) to study the effectiveness of a computer generated tachistoscope-like program. Though they noticed some positive changes, their data did not support this method. Current research on these devices and programs could not be found, and this type of intervention is likely no longer used.

McBride (1974) and Olson (1975) took a different approach by exploring rapid reading techniques similar to those for teaching print readers. In general, participants who were involved in these studies were able to increase their reading rates. Recommendations from Olson emphasized the need for incorporating reading techniques into the beginning instructional program for braille readers (as explained further in Chapter 4), the value of multiple finger use and independent hand movement in braille reading, as well as the need for further research on rapid braille reading.

While updated research on rapid braille reading could not be found, results from the ABC Braille Study support Olson's recommendation of multiple finger use and independent hand movement (Wright et al., 2009). A subset of data suggested, "participants who used a two-handed reading pattern increased their reading speed at a greater rate than did the participants who used a one-handed reading pattern" (Wright et al., 2009, p. 688). Wright et al. noted that individuals who initially learned a one-handed reading approach were less likely to incorporate their second hand, thus limiting their ability to use more efficient two-handed reading patterns. As a result, they recommend for teachers of students who are blind or visually impaired to introduce a two-handed reading approach to beginning braille readers. The authors also concluded that, while it may be logical to introduce contracted braille when students are older and can comprehend the complexities, there was no significant data to support this hypothesis (Wright et al., 2009). "No statistically significant coorelation was noted between the number of contractions that were introduced and inefficient or efficient characteristics" or that "readers who used contracted braille had more difficulty recognizing characters" (p. 659).

Other factors that are believed to positively influence reading rate are early braille introduction (Stanfa & Johnson, 2015, Trent & Truan, 1997), daily or frequent braille practice (Stanfa & Johnson, 2015, Trent & Truan, 1997), and reading strategies adapted from print literacy instruction (Stanfa & Johnson, 2015, Holbrook et al., 2017). Two commonly used reading strategies to increase reading speed are repeated reading and paired reading (Holbrook et al., 2017). An individual's reading rates may vary depending on their reading task. Knowlton and Wetzel (1996) found that reading rates in adult braille readers varied across four different scenarios: oral reading, scanning, studying, and silent reading. These findings were later affirmed by Knowlton and Wetzel in a follow-up study (2000).

Common Instructional Approaches to Braille

There has been an ongoing conversation and debate among teaching professionals about whether young children should initially learn how to read and write using uncontracted braille or contracted braille (D'Andrea, 2009). This debate was one of the driving questions behind the ABC Braille Study. After following and assessing the development of literacy skills in young beginning braille readers over a five year period (2002–2007), researchers concluded an early introduction to contractions has a minor correlation with stronger reading skills and higher literacy performance (Wall Emerson et al., 2009). A troubling result from the study indicated most students learning braille fell behind their sighted peers in reading skills. To combat this problem, Wall Emerson et al. recommended a "focus on reading processes, regardless of the specifics of how the braille is introduced" (2009, p. 622).

There are many different philosophies and methodologies on how to teach reading. Some examples include: the basal reader approach, the phonetic approach, the linguistic approach, the language experience approach, and the modified alphabet approach. Lowenfeld (1973) recommends that teachers be cognizant of all approaches so that appropriate systems can be adapted or combined to accommodate individual children.

While there are multiple approaches to teaching reading and writing, Swenson (2016) explains there are a few critical components to a successful literacy program. These components include read alouds, opportunities for sustained reading and writing of connected text, high quality reading materials, access to a variety of texts, access to a large quantity of reading material, authentic opportunities to use reading and writing, social interaction during literacy activities, and instruction that provides the right amount of challenge for each student. Swenson noted that this balanced approach to literacy is beneficial for both print and braille users.

Researchers and teachers in the field have compiled books and braille programs to support the teaching and learning of braille reading and writing. Below is a list of resources for reference:

Curriculum

- *Braille FUNdamentals: UEB* (tsbvi.edu/store/) by Shannon Darst, edited by Margaret Edwards (2021)
  Braille FUNdamentals is a program designed for teaching the Unified English Braille code. It is divided into four different levels: primary, upper elementary, middle school, and high school. Lessons include a variety of listening, literature, reading, and writing activities.

- *Braille Too: The Next Generation* (brl2.com/the-next-generation) by Sharon K. Cross-Coquillette
  Braille Too: The Next Generation is an extensively revised UEB edition of the *Braille Too* reading and writing program originally created by Nancy Lake Hepker and Sharon Cross-Coquillette.

  Braille Too: The Next Generation is designed for middle- and high-school students. The program is available on a flash drive, which allows teachers to emboss the pages they need, use the program with an electronic braille display, and customize it for individual student needs. The program also incudes large print exercises, making it accessible for dual media learners (print and braille).

- *Building on Patterns: Primary Braille Literacy Program* (aph.bop.org) by American Printing House for the Blind
  Building on Patterns is a literacy program for individuals learning braille. It is designed to not only teach the braille code, but also all components of language arts including phonemic awareness, phones, comprehension, fluency, and vocabulary. *Building on Patterns* addresses language development, sound discrimination, tactual discrimination, and concept development.

- *Mangold Braille Program: Basic Braille* (exceptionalteaching.com/mangold-basic-braille-program-kit-units-1-2/) by Sally Mangold
  The *Basic Braille* program formerly known as the *Mangold Developmental Program* of *Tactile Perception and Braille Letter Recognition* is designed for beginning braille readers. It focuses on tactile discrimination, proper hand position, and tracking and provides an introduction to the letters of the alphabet. The *Mangold Program* has been expanded beyond the original kit and has additional units that can be used to teach braille contractions.

- *Braille Brain: A Braille Training Program for Educators and Family Members* (pathstoliteracy.org/braille-brain/braille-training-program) by Kim Blackwell, Cheryl Kamei-Hannan, & Gina Michell, 2021.

Braille Brain is a training program funded by the United States Department of Education, Rehabilitation Services Agency, (H235E190002). The overall goal of the project is to promote literacy and STEM instruction provided by pre-service and in-service teachers of students with visual impairments, paraprofessionals, parents, and educational team members.

- *UEB Online* (uebonline.org) by NextSense Institute
  UEB Online is a fully online braille training program designed for educators, families, allied health professionals, education administrators, and policy makers. It includes self-paced lessons divided into four categories: UEB Literacy, UEB Introductory Mathematics, UEB Advanced Mathematics, and UEB Extension Mathematics. The website is accessible for people with visual impairments and could be used by high school braille students who want more practice with braille and to learn UEB for technical materials.

Books

- *Beginning with Braille: Firsthand Experiences with a Balanced Approach to Literacy* by Anna M. Swenson (2016)
- *Braille Literacy: A Functional Approach* by Diane P. Wormsley (2004)
- *Instructional Strategies for Braille Literacy*, edited by Diane P. Wormsley and Frances Mary D'Andrea (1997)
- *Foundations of Braille Literacy* by Evelyn J. Rex, Alan J. Koenig, Diane P. Wormsley, and Robert L. Baker (1994)
- *Foundations of Education Volume II: Instructional Strategies for Teaching Children and Youths with Visual Impairments* edited by M. Cay Holbrook, Cheryl Kamei-Hannan, and Tessa McCarthy (2017)
- *Guidelines and Games for Teaching Efficient Braille Reading* by Myrna R. Olson in collaboration with Sally S. Mangold (First Edition, 1981); by Renae Bjorg and Myrna R. Olson (Second Edition, 2021)
- *I-M-ABLE: Individual Meaning Centered Approach to Braille Literacy Education* by Diane P. Wormsley (2016)
- *Reading Connections: Strategies for Teaching Students with Visual Impairments* by Cheryl Kamei-Hannan and Leila Ansari Ricci (2015)

References

Bickford, J. O., & Falco, R. A. (2012). Technology for early braille literacy: Comparison of traditional braille instruction and instruction with an electronic notetaker. *Journal of Visual Impairment & Blindness, 106*(10), 679–693. https://doi.org/10.1177/0145482X1210601012

Braille Authority of North America. (2012, November). *BANA adopts Unified English Braille for United States* [Press Release]. https://brailleauthority.org/pressreleases/pr-2012november.html

Braille Translation Software from Duxbury Systems. Retrieved April 20, 2021, from https://duxburysystems.com

Cates, D. L., & Sowell, V. M. (1990). Using a braille tachistoscope to improve braille reading speed. *Journal of Visual Impairment & Blindness, 84*(10), 556–559.

D'Andrea, F. M. (2009). A history of instructional methods in uncontracted and contracted braille. *Journal of Visual Impairment & Blindness, 103*(10), 585–594. https://doi.org/10.1177/0145482X0910301003.

Grunwald, A. (1967). A braille-reading machine. *Science*. https://doi.org/10.1126/science.154.3745.144

Hanninen, K. (1975) *Teaching the visually handicapped*. Charles Merrill Publishing Company.

Heber, R. (1967). *A study of programmed instruction in braille* (ED15303). ERIC. https://eric.ed.gov/?q=ED015303&id=ED015303

International Council on English Braille (ICEB) Unified English Braille (UEB). Retrieved April 19, 2021, from https://iceb.org/ueb.html

Jameson, M. (1966). The optophone: Its beginning and development. *Bulletin of Prosthetic Research*, 25–28.

Kederis, C. (1971). *Training for increasing braille reading rates* (ED023229). ERIC.

Knowlton, M., & Wetzel, R. (1996). Braille reading rates as a function of reading tasks. *Journal of Visual Impairment & Blindness, 90*(3), 227–236. https://doi.org/10.1177/0145482X9609000312

Knowlton, M., & Wetzel, R. (2000). A comparison of print and braille reading rates on three reading tasks. *Journal of Visual Impairment & Blindness, 94*(3), 146–154. https://doi.org/10.1177/0145482X0009400303

Lowenfeld, B., Abel, G., & Hatlen, P. (1969) *Blind children learn to read*. Charles C. Thomas.

Millar, S. (1987). The perceptual "window" in two-handed braille: Do the left and right hands process text simultaneously? *Cortex, 23*, 111–122.

McBride, V. (1974) Exploration of rapid reading in braille. *New Look for the Blind, 68*(1), 8–13.

Michaelson, K. J., Matz, L. & Morgan, D. (2015). Using a new electronic brailler to improve braille learning at the Florida School for the Deaf and Blind. *Journal of Visual Impairment & Blindness, 109*(3), 226–231. https://doi.org/10.1177/0145482X1510900308

Braille Authority of North America. (2012, November 2) Motion to Adopt UEB. https://brailleauthority.org/ueb/UEBpassed.html

National Library Service for the Blind and Print Disabled Library of Congress (2020). Retrieved April 20, 2021, from https://loc.gov/nls/resources/blindness-and-vision-impairment/devices-aids/braille-embossers/

Nolan, C. (1966). *Reading and listening in learning by the blind: Progress report.* American Printing House for the Blind.

Olson, M. (1975). *The effects of training in rapid reading on the reading rate and comprehension of braille and large print readers.* University Microfilms International.

Orr, D., Friedman, H., & Williams, J. (1965). Trainability of listening comprehension of speeded discourse. *Journal of Educational Psychology, 56*(3), 148–156. https://doi.org/10.1037/h0021987

Risjord, C. (2014). *The ABCs of UEB: A Guide for the transition from English Braille American Edition (EBAE) to the Rules of Unified English Braille (UEB).* Braille Authority of North America.

Rosner, Y., & Perlman, A. (2018). The effect of the usage of computer-based assistive devices on the functioning and quality of life of individuals who are blind or have low vision. *Journal of Visual Impairment & Blindness, 112*(1), 87–99. https://doi.org/10.1177/0145482X1811200108

Sapp, W., & Hatlen, P. (2010). The expanded core curriculum: Where we have been, where we are going, and how we can get there. *Journal of Visual Impairment & Blindness, 104*(6), 338–348. https://doi.org/10.1177/0145482X1010400604

Swenson, A. M. (2016). *Beginning with braille: First hand experiences with a balanced approach to literacy (2nd ed.).* AFB Press.

Trent, S. D., & Truan, M. B. (1997). Speed, accuracy, and comprehension of adolescent braille readers in a specialized school. *Journal of Visual Impairment & Blindness, 91*(5), 494–500. https://doi.org/10.1177/0145482X9709100509

Wall Emerson, R., Holbrook, M. C., & D'Andrea, F. M. (2009). Acquisition of literacy skills by young children who are blind: Results from the ABC Braille Study. *Journal of Visual Impairment & Blindness, 103*(10), 610–624.

Wright, T., Wormsley, D. P., & Kamei-Hannan, C. (2009). Hand movements and braille reading efficiency: Data from the Alphabetic Braille and Contracted Study. *Journal of Visual Impairment & Blindness, 103*(10), 649–661. https://doi.org/10.1177/0145482X0910301008

CHAPTER 3

Preschool Experiences Important to Emergent Braille Readers

The Development of Emergent Literacy Skills

When assessing any child's readiness to read, the teacher must consider such factors as mental age, physical maturation, social-emotional development, experiential background, oral language skills, sensory acuity, sensory efficiency, and motivation. Young children with severe visual impairments have limited access and exposure to examples of literacy within their environments, limiting their development of language and literacy skills (Chen, 2014, p. 548). To promote emergent literacy skills in children with visual impairments, the focus of instruction in a preschool experience should be on the development of skills in four areas: (a) early sensory-motor abilities; (b) sensory acuity and efficiency; (c) basic concepts; and (d) reading awareness.

It is the purpose of this chapter to discuss and provide specific suggestions for the development of emergent literacy skills in each of these areas to parents and preschool teachers of children who are visually impaired. Literacy-related behaviors occurring in the preschool period are legitimate and important aspects of literacy (Whitehurst & Lonigan, 1998, pp. 848–849).

Early Sensory Motor Abilities

Sensory and motor development is the gradual process beginning at birth when the child gains use and coordination of their body. The child also begins to understand, make sense of, and react appropriately to information gathered from their environment through the seven sensory systems (Allman, 2014, p. 118). There are five systems that provide information about the world outside the body: vision, hearing (auditory system), touch (tactile system), taste (gustatory system), and smell (olfactory system). In addition, there are two internal senses that provide information about the movement, position, and stabilization of the body. The *proprioceptive sense* provides information about position and movements of the body. The *vestibular sense* detects changes in the direction of gravitational pull and influences balance, movement, and posture. When one sensory system is impaired, the efficiency of other sensory systems become more important. Adults need to create access to sensory information during early development, since these experiences provide the foundation for development and learning.

Human Attachment

The learning process begins with a child's interaction with their environment. Human attachment is typically the first step of this interaction. While infants with sight have the advantage of visually tracking or focusing upon their caregivers, infants who are visually impaired must find a tactile-auditory language that will bring them into this first human partnership. Because children who are visually impaired cannot depend on visual input to gather information, they rely on the use of other sensory mechanisms such as hearing, touch, smell, and taste. It is essential that caregivers talk to infants who are visually impaired, verbalizing their interactions using rich detail and descriptions with them during bathing, feeding, diapering, and dressing (Steinman, 2006). A caring and loving touch from another human is a necessary part of developing attachment and communication. When a baby's cry is responded to in a quick and warm manner, the child develops a bond or attachment to the caregiver, while developing their tactual sense. This trust is carried over to an instructor who guides the hands of a child who is visually impaired when exploring their environment (Newton, 2000).

Caregivers of infants who are visually impaired should expect motor development to progress at a slower pace than for infants with sight. While a child with sight usually learns to lift their head from prone by 1 month of age, a child with visual impairment lacks the visual stimulation to do this. Placing an infant on their stomach for short periods of time while awake and supervised helps the infant develop neck and trunk strength. As the child develops arm and trunk stability, they will move to support themselves into and out of prone positioning, adding rotational movements (Texas School for the Blind and Visually Impaired). These early gross and fine motor activities help a child sit unsupported and develop better hand strength, which allows for pushing the keys of a Perkins Brailler.

Although it is important to introduce sound to the infant who is visually impaired, it must be understood that they will be unable to localize it until they are about 9 months old. Subsequent skills of sitting, standing, and walking alone may also occur late for children who are visually impaired. This delay exists not only because there is no visual stimulation to motivate these activities, but also because the development of balance is more difficult to achieve without the visual sense.

Discovery of Objects

Because infants who are visually impaired cannot use sound as an adaptive substitute for vision until they are about 9 months old, babies who are visually impaired need to be deliberately introduced to toys. Toys need to be presented in a limited space and should be tactually and auditorily interesting. Toys introduced at the midline, with some physical guidance of the child's hands to explore them, will also be important. Handclap games provide verbal stimulation to accompany midline play and develop body awareness concepts. These games also encourage sitting balance, as the hands are being used for play and not balancing. Rattles, rainsticks, and other grasping activity toys should be placed directly into the hands of visually impaired children, allowing them to work on the palmar, or grasping, reflex. Helping them shake the rattle in order to produce sound will assist in forming the sense of cause and effect. Activity gyms and playmats are multisensory, utilizing engaging sounds and a variety of tactual fabrics.

As soon as infants who are visually impaired sit unsupported, an infant seat with a tray may be helpful for placing favorite toys in front of them for tactual exploration. A play yard also provides a limited safe space to explore tactually interesting toys and books, especially for children ages 8 to 12 months who are becoming more mobile. A child may also benefit from the "Little Room" (Nielsen, 1992), a space that can be constructed from plexiglass wall modules from which play objects are suspended. Generally speaking, toys that are pushed give infants who are visually impaired a better sense of their bodies with respect to objects than do pull toys. Household items, nesting toys, rhythm instruments, and music boxes are additional favorites among children who are visually impaired.

Children without vision need assistance and longer periods of time to compare the sizes and shapes of objects in their environment. Whenever possible, parents should permit free exploration of at least one cupboard or drawer to enhance such generalizations. Children with sight quickly determine the use of objects through visual observation. Caregivers and preschool teachers of children with visual impairments must deliberately show object function and further help the children distinguish between "real" objects and "models" or representations.

Locomotion
Individual differences in the early development process are based on timing, not in the sequence. Early development progresses in an orderly fashion, and developmental "norms" are based on when most children achieve milestone skills within a range. Children who are visually impaired will gain the strength and coordination for locomotion, creeping and crawling, though it might take a little longer. Caregivers will naturally worry about the safety of their child who is visually impaired. It will be important to guard against the resulting temptation to overprotect. A reasonably safe play space should be fenced off for the child's independent exploration. Stairs should be blocked using secure baby gates. Sharp objects and heavy objects that are easily tipped may be removed or secured, but minor falls and bumps should not be prevented. Since motor movements may not be initiated by children who are visually impaired, caregivers and preschool teachers will have to manipulate them into movement from birth. Activity jumpers, walkers, and bouncing chairs help these infants safely release pent-up tension and energy. Through movement, children develop gross and fine motor skills.

Sensory Acuity and Efficiency
When the visual sense is functioning with a high degree of efficiency and combined with touch, the two senses are used in combination by children to build the concepts that establish their understanding of the world. Vision alone, even when it is unimpaired, is not sufficient for the development of perceptual skills. Tactile information must be combined with vision for a period of time before these qualities can be perceived using vision alone

(Allman, 2014, p. 123). Children who are visually impaired, on the other hand, may need to rely more heavily on other senses, while developing the visual sense as supplementary. Although the tactile and auditory channels are the two most vital to the reader of braille, the development of acuity and efficiency in all sensory channels will be discussed. The rationale for this is that a child who is visually impaired relates to the braille symbols on a page to the extent they can extract meaning. Furthermore, meaning is expanded as the braille reader has more experiences and when their ability to integrate experiences is achieved through all sensory channels.

Kinesthetic-Tactile Learning

In order to learn during kinesthetic-tactile learning, materials are touched and manipulated. Children are actively engaged by using their entire body to carry out physical activities and movements, producing multisensory learning, rather than only hands-on learning.

Berthold Lowenfeld, a well-known and respected former director of research for the American Foundation for the Blind, believed babies have two main sources of stimulation for "skin senses" during their first few weeks of life—the reflexive movement of their individual bodies and the touch and tender handling of those caring for them (1973). In an infant who is visually impaired, manipulation of the limbs causes the kinesthetic receptors to provide information about body space and the possibilities of movement within that space. Previously, it was believed such manipulation was received passively at the unconscious perceptual level, but storage of motor patterns may contribute to later cognitive development. Literature now suggests both conscious and unconscious perceptions of position and movement are considered under one sense: proprioception (Allman, 2014, p. 121).

Because infants who are visually impaired cannot visually guide their hands to explore the environment and have not developed voluntary grasp reactions, initial planned stimulation must be provided. Therefore, the adults in the children's environments must give physical guidance using hand-under-hand guidance during exploration, verbally describe differences among things they touch, and provide textures that are soft and warm to the touch to encourage further exploration. Before they start to explore with their hands, infants gain a wide variety of information through their mouths. Thus, it is essential that children who are visually impaired have opportunities to safely explore with their mouth foods of different consistencies and flavors, as well as objects, which are pleasing and safe. Caregivers and preschool teachers should experiment with the tactual preferences of infants who are visually impaired and gradually introduce new textures to arouse their interest.

Children learn in many ways. Caregivers and preschool teachers can carry out the following multisensory tactual activities with preschoolers who are visually impaired.

- Present toys that are tactually pleasant and not too small to examine or grasp.

- Encourage play with nesting toys such as cardboard boxes, barrels, measuring cups, and spoons, starting with large items and working toward the smaller ones.
- Introduce toys that require fine motor manipulations: busy boxes, work benches, wind-up toys, keys and locks, and large nuts and bolts.
- In guiding tactual exploration, give the child word names and action verbs to accompany the actions.
- Help the child manipulate their own body, followed by the body of a doll or another person while verbally describing qualities of objects as well as the action verbs to accompany their movement.
- Encourage independent dressing, and teach the child to manipulate clothing fasteners such as buttons, hooks, and zippers.
- Play copycat games for bead stringing, gradually reducing the size of the beads.
- Create touch and feel letters and felt letter boards.
- Glue materials to a deck of playing cards and have the child match pairs according to texture; make initial pairs grossly different (e.g., sandpaper, wool, plastic, flannel).
- Create a sensory bin: a rice-filled bin with toys and objects to match sensory attributes and sounds.
- Give the child a number of containers with matching lids to open.
- Give the child modeling dough, clay, slime, or finger paints to manipulate.
- Write using a rainbow salt tray: place a rainbow-colored piece of paper in the bottom of a tray with edges covered in a layer of salt, and use the fingers to write letters or words.
- Spray shaving cream into a sensory tray or in a baggie and add objects to tactually explore.
- Brush teeth and encourage bathing with minimal assistance.
- Introduce cutting and pasting. Have the child make a "touch scrapbook" of interesting textures and shapes.
- When taking a walk, have the child identify differences among walking surfaces such as sidewalk, dirt, grass, and pavement.
- Introduce three-dimensional geometric figures; make raised-line drawings of them for the child to explore, and have the child make a raised-line interpretation of a shape.

American Printing House for the Blind has a number of items that support teaching texture and tactile discrimination, such as:

- *Color-By-Texture Marking Mats*
- *Flip-Over Concept Books: TEXTURES*
- *Giant Textured Beads With and Without Pattern Matching Cards*
- *Peg Kit*
- *Puzzle Form Board Kit*
- *Sensory Cylinder Set*
- *Shape Board*
- *Spangle Tangle: Play and Explore Kit*
- *Textured Matching Blocks*
- *Textured Pegs*
- *Textured Sorting Circles and Shapes*
- *On the Way to Literacy* storybooks with real objects and textures

Auditory Sense

Stimulation of the auditory sense is important for children who are visually impaired even before they are able to use their tactual-kinesthetic senses. During early infancy, infants can already differentiate their mother's voice from other voices. At the end of the first year, the child can associate a sound in their environment with a function or specific event (Allman, 2014, p. 128). It is of great importance for the development of auditory discrimination skills that sounds and their sources be introduced early in the course of daily routines. When appropriate, the child should have the opportunity to visually and tactually explore the source of the sound. A tactual-auditory dialogue forms a basis for the child's learning and helps them establish a perceptual frame of reference. If the auditory stimulation provided does not give meaningful information, the child remains at a mechanical level of sound reception. Too often children who are visually impaired are left alone to be stimulated by noise (e.g., radio, television) and consequently learn rote repetition of words, phrases, and jingles. A child who is visually impaired needs frequent vocal stimulation and interaction, first with adults and then with other children. Clarification of auditory perceptions comes through others listening to their responses and by answering questions about themselves and the environment.

Because the only information available to an aural reader is in one time dimension, a sound cannot be recalled for consideration once it has passed. Unless the words are remembered, processed, and coded as heard, the reader's perception may be inaccurate, distorted, or completely meaningless. Even though aural reading offers many advantages to children who are visually impaired, far more attention should be given to gathering the specific information needed from the passage with the most efficient use of time and as few external prompts as possible (Holbrook, 2017, p. 419). Auditory-based technology tools for literacy and travel skills have provided greater access, specifically, for individuals with visual impairments. This technology includes live or recorded human readers, talking calculators, screen readers, digital or audiobooks, personal music devices, and electronic notetakers with speech access (Holbrook, 2017, p. 602). Advances in screen-reading software allow the user to control the reading episode and navigate through passages moving ahead and back, while being able to change the speed of the reader and quality of speech (Holbrook, 2017, p. 420).

Below is a list of developmental activities to be carried out by caregivers and teachers wishing to enhance auditory readiness and efficiency of preschoolers who are visually impaired (Willings; Auditory Readiness).

- Limit exposure to "artificial sounds" of television and radio; play quiet relaxing music in the background.
- Talk to the child using language rich in details.
- Locate a noise stimulus, and encourage the child to reach for and move toward the sound.
- Choose toys or sound producers that are age appropriate, and continue introducing new sound toys.
- Play hide and seek, calling to the child from various directions.
- Have the child touch noise-making household items—toilet, faucet, drawers, crinkling paper, vacuum, refrigerator, clock, furnace—and reproduce sounds they make.
- Take neighborhood walks pointing to sounds such as cars, dogs, toys, wind, and trees; then, ask the child what they hear.
- Take field trips to a variety of stores, zoos, farms, and other places to hear new environmental sounds.
- Play word games with the child using animal sounds.
- Encourage the child to imitate sounds they hear.
- Perform body movements to music, responding to sounds that are loud versus soft in tone, high versus low in pitch, fast versus slow in tempo.
- Point out how sounds differ when listened to from inside versus outside; expose them to constant versus intermittent sound.
- Discuss the importance of sound for safety purposes, including fire alarms, sirens, and weather emergencies.

Visual Sense

In addition to the sequential development of visual abilities, efforts should be made to help children use any vision efficiently. Visual efficiency skills help children prepare for learning and safe and efficient travel. Children who are visually impaired can be challenged with developing eye-hand coordination. Body movements are difficult to coordinate in response to what is seen. Students who are visually impaired may need motivators and assistance developing motor milestones through the use of visual and auditory cues. Students can independently adjust their body, head, and eyes to encourage fixation or direct a gaze and hold an object steadily in view. Once they are able to attend to a single object at near range, introduce objects and people at other distances. Then introduce multiple items at one time, and encourage shifting of the gaze from one object or person to another. Once the child is able to visually attend to objects and materials in their environment, they can be encouraged to visually track, or maintain visual attention on an object, as long as the object is moving. Visually scanning is a skill that differs from visual tracking in that scanning requires the student to view an area to locate an item or information as opposed to maintaining visual contact while an object or person moves from one place to another. Visual tracking skills are vital to the success of reading. Students must be able to move their eyes accurately in order to read across a line of print. Visual discrimination skills are also needed to learn to read print, recognizing details in visual images such as shapes, colors, and position of objects, people, and printed materials. Having the ability to notice details without getting confused by the background is *figure-ground perception*. If a child has difficulty with visual closure, it will be challenging to identify an object or picture when part of the object is absent. Visual association is used to sort and classify items that belong together but are not identical. Visual memory and visual imagery are two visual efficiency skills important for academics and developing good orientation and mobility skills. *Visual memory* is the ability to store and retrieve information that has been seen previously and is no longer present. *Visual imagery* is information that passes through the brain as though something is being perceived when nothing is actually happening.

It is possible vision will not be the most viable mode for learning. The use of optical and nonoptical supports can be used to support any visual ability the child has in the most efficient manner (Holbrook, 2017, p. 598). Optical supports include low vision devices that fall into categories of near vision magnification, distance vision magnification, and electronic magnification. Nonoptical supports fall into the general categories of child and material positioning, color, contrast, size, distance, lighting, and visual array.

Olfactory and Gustatory Sense
The sense of smell and taste often work in unison and contribute to the general mood, nutritional health, and information gathering for the child who is visually impaired (Holbrook, 2017, p. 603). When using the sense of smell, the information goes directly to the limbic system, where emotions are evoked in the brain. Certain smells can influence a child's behavior positively or negatively depending on the experience attached to the smell. Smells can capture a child's attention and signal the onset of an activity. The scent of toothpaste indicates it is time for the child to brush their teeth. The pleasant scent of the child's mother's perfume or lotion can trigger powerful memories. Certain

smells support nutrition, indicating it is time to eat. Foods that smell pleasant are more likely to be explored by children who are visually impaired.

The texture of food also plays a critical role in developing taste for new foods. Children should be introduced to a variety of textures and tastes that can be labeled as sweet, salty, bitter, sour, and savory. Ambient scents in the environment can be avoided so more discrete odors can be used for information (Allman, 2014, p. 129). Caregivers and teachers need to indicate smells in the house, school, or neighborhood that will serve to supplement the child's knowledge of the environment. Scents can be helpful as identifying information for particular locations. For example, the smell of laundry detergent and fabric softener indicates the laundry room or laundromat, while freshly cut grass indicates the outdoors. Safety factors tied to smell (e.g., the smell of gas, burning) should be discussed as soon as children are old enough to understand. Attention should be paid to the possible negative effects odors and tastes may have on children who are visually impaired. Some children are hypersensitive to scents and may react negatively; other scents are a distraction to the child.

Basic Concept Development

Basic concept development is the process of understanding the characteristics of an item and understanding the relationship of the item's characteristics among other objects in the environment (Allman, 2014, p. 18). Unlike children with sight who attain good concept development through incidental learning, children who are visually impaired lack incidental learning and must have concepts specifically taught to them (Sacks, 2016, p. 190). The following are 10 categories of concept development that must be understood by children with visual impairments: actions, quantity, reasoning, emotional and social awareness, and awareness of the body, environment, object characteristics, symbols, time, and space.

In general, for each concept, children progress through three levels of attainment (Allman, 2014, p. 64). The first level is described as *concrete*, at which point children consider the physical properties of an object. The second level considers the *functional* aspect of the item or concept. The *abstract* level, the highest level of attainment, is reached when children are able to generalize from the concrete and functional an understanding of the major attributes of the concept. Handling an object is generally inadequate for establishing its depth, intricacy, or totality. Children with visual impairments lack the visual sense, which serves to "unify" and establish the wholeness of objects at a distance. They tend to learn in a "part-to-whole" manner, experiencing individual parts of the world and then learning how to put the parts together in a meaningful way through tactual manipulation. Children with sight tend to learn in "whole-to-part," meaning they understand the big picture before attending to the details (Sacks, 2016, p. 182). Children who are visually impaired take much longer to develop at the abstract level. Abstract concepts often involve items that cannot be touched or physically explored. Ask questions, ensuring the child understands the concepts involved.

Allman and Lewis (2014, p. 64) outlined the following four-step process to help children develop an understanding of concepts once the child is aware the item exists:

1. Being aware of the item (e.g., a plate)
2. Having a desire to interact with the item (eating off a plate), and being given the opportunity to do so
3. Labeling the item ("The plate is round.") and having multiple experiences interacting with various forms of the item (plastic plates, ceramic plates, dinner plates, salad plates)
4. Classifying other items with similar characterstics that relate to the item (serving platters, soup bowls, pasta bowls, and serving bowls)

Ways of Teaching Specific Concepts to Preschoolers

The *Boehm-3 Test of Basic Concepts* is a good assessment instrument for determining which concepts children who are visually impaired have mastered before entering school. Each item in the test has been adapted for use with children who are visually impaired. Students will learn concepts best through actual, direct, hands-on experiences with real objects. Whenever possible, objects closely related to the child—parts of their body, clothing, toys, furniture, and utensils—should be used when teaching basic concepts. Children with visual impairments need to be actively involved in learning about their environment and the objects within it. Through this, they can receive direct sensory impressions and repeated contact with items in the environment, which reinforces their learning and helps them integrate information into the concepts they are developing (Allman, 2014, p. 149).

Carmen Willings (2017) outlines concepts to teach through guided exploration and explanations, including:

- Objects: chair, table, paper, book, etc.
- Shapes: square, triangle, circle, rectangle, cylinder, cube, curve, oval, etc.
- Sizes: big, little, tall, short, thick, thin, wide, narrow, etc.
- Textures: rough, smooth, bumpy, soft, hard, furry, sticky, fuzzy, slick, etc.
- Body Awareness: parts, functions, and movements.
- Positions and Spatial Relationships: on, off, in, out, front, back, left, right, up, down, above, below, top, bottom, in front, behind, on top, underneath, next to, beside, through, middle, center, between, here, there, under, over, upside down, right side up, first, last, together, apart, forward, behind, sideways, straight, there, etc.

Reading Awareness

Children with sight become aware of written words long before they are able to read them. Children who are visually impaired, however, do not receive the same type of early exposure to braille. By law, the Individuals with Disabilities Education Act (IDEA) states all children who are visually impaired must be considered candidates for instruction in braille, unless a team of professionals determines that braille would be an inappropriate literacy medium (Allman, 2014, p. 584). If braille is or will be a child's literacy medium, the family needs to be committed to learning along with the child. Parents and teachers need to make deliberate efforts to expose children who are visually impaired to braille in many varied, positive ways.

Modeling Good Braille Reading

Provide a braille-rich environment. Just as children with sight are exposed to print through reading materials, children who are visually impaired need to be exposed to braille materials and other tactually interesting storybook props, counting manipulatives, puzzles, and textured blocks. There are many literacy-related teachable moments. Draw the child's attention to braille in an elevator and on signs and examine a braille menu in a restaurant. Provide favorite books that have been adapted with braille. Write braille notes, cards, and letters for the child.

Labeling Objects with Braille

Label belongings and other household items familiar to the child who is visually impaired. Braille labels should be attached in strategic locations for the child who is visually impaired to explore. If they will be facing the object (e.g., a door), the label should be upright at the approximate reach of the child. Labels that might be read by reaching down (e.g., back of the chair), should be affixed upside down in order to read right side up to the child's touch. Furthermore, the words used to label these objects should be those the child uses (e.g., the proper name of a favorite toy). It is a good idea if labels are written in contracted braille, since this is what children will encounter in school. To promote sharing with sighted members of the family, the corresponding print should be provided with each braille label. Each new label should be introduced to the child by guiding their fingers across the word in the proper direction first. Without forcing the issue, subtly reference the concept of starting from the beginning indicator of each word.

Providing Memorized Material in Braille

Nursery rhymes, short poems, songs, and television commercials are often memorized by young children. Children who are visually impaired should be given the braille corresponding to memorized material and, in this way, be introduced to the "feeling" of continuous braille reading.

Summary

This chapter was written on the premise that in the areas related to reading readiness, children who are visually impaired develop differently than children with sight. Parents and preschool teachers need to make more deliberate efforts to develop and refine sensory abilities in children who are visually impaired than are necessary for children with sight. The environment must be brought to the child who is visually impaired in an organized, consistent, and meaningful way. Concepts should be taught in a similar fashion. Understanding of basic concepts need to stem from a child's personal interaction with the environment, rather than from rote memorization of verbal definitions. Finally, exposure to the braille medium must occur as early in the lives of children who are visually impaired as exposure to print occurs for children with sight. Not only must preschool children who are visually impaired become aware of braille as a means of communication, they must also have enough positive experiences with it to be sufficiently motivated to learn how to understand it.

References

Allman, C., & Lewis, S. (2014). *ECC Essentials: Teaching the expanded core curriculum to students with visual impairments.* American Foundation for the Blind.

American Printing House. (2021). Instructional Products Catalog 2020–2021. https://nyc3.digitaloceanspaces.com/aph/app/uploads/2020/06/091349

Chen, Deborah. (2014). *Essential Elements in Early Intervention: Visual Impairment and Multiple Disabilities.* American Foundation for the Blind.

Holbrook, M. C., Kamei-Hannan, C., & McCarthy, T. (2017). *Foundations of education, third edition, volume II: Instructional strategies for teaching children and youths with visual impairments.* American Foundation for the Blind.

Lowenfeld, B. (1973). *The visually handicapped child in school.* John Day Company.

Nielsen, L. (1992). *Space and Self: Active Learning by Means of the Little Room.* Sikon.

Newton, G. (2000). The importance of touch in parent-infant bonding. *See/Hear.* https:// tsbvi.edu/seehear/fall00/infantbonding.htm

Office of Disability Rights, District of Columbia. (2006). *People first language: Usage guidelines.* Retrieved July, 2021, from https://odr.dc.gov/page/people-first-language

Olson, M. R., & Mangold, S. (1981). Guidelines and Games for Teaching Efficient Braille Reading. American Printing House for the Blind.

Sacks, S. Z., & Zatta, M. C. (2016). *Keys to educational success: Teaching students with multiple impairments and multiple disabilities.* American Foundation for the Blind.

Steinman, B. A., LeJeune, B. J., & Kimbrough, B. T. (2006). Developmental stages of reading processes in children who are blind and sighted. *Journal of Visual Impairment & Blindness.* American Foundation for the Blind.

Texas School for the Blind and Visually Impaired. (2015). *ECI gross motor movement.* Retrieved August, 2021 from https://tsbvi.edu/early-childhood/1925-eci-gross-motor-movement

Whitehurst, G., & Lonigan, C. (1998). Child Development and Emergent Literacy. *Child Development*, 69(3), 848–872. https://doi.org/10.2307/1132208

Willings, C. Auditory Readiness. *Teaching Students with Visual Impairments*. Retrieved June, 2021, from https://teachingvisuallyimpaired.com/auditory-readiness.html

Willings, C. (2017, October 28), Concepts to Teach. *Teaching Students with Visual Impairments*. Retrieved June, 2021, from https://teachingvisuallyimpaired.com/concepts-to-teach.html

Willings, C. (2019, June 9) Visual Efficiency Skills. *Teaching Students with Visual Impairments*. Retrieved June, 2021, from https://teachingvisuallyimpaired.com/visual-efficiency-skills.html

CHAPTER 4

Activities for Teaching Braille More Efficiently at the Beginning Level

Exciting news! He tapes the braille he does at school on his headboard. He is proud of his work.

—Parent of a kindergarten student

Incorporation of Rapid Reading Principles

This chapter suggests ways that rapid reading principles might be brought into the teaching of beginning braille reading. *Beginning reading*, as used here, means instruction through Grade 3. Regardless of age, however, readers who are newly blind, learning braille, and consequently reading at these levels, might also be helped by activities in this chapter. Studies of braille reading strongly suggest that frequently observed undesirable braille reading behaviors may be prevented if the initial instruction focuses primarily on good reading habits, rather than on decoding skills (Bloom, 1974; Douglas and Mangold, 1975). Once the mechanics of braille reading are mastered, the student can devote all of their energy toward more complex skills and perform at a higher level of reading accuracy. Through the application of rapid reading techniques, the mechanics of braille reading can be mastered more efficiently (Umsted, 1972; Wallace, 1973; McBride, 1974; Olson, 1975).

The incorporation of rapid reading principles into beginning braille instruction does not constitute a total "reading approach," but it can serve as an adjunct to the current reading methods. In this chapter, a discussion for breaking down the reading process into various skills is presented. A certain amount of overlap cannot be avoided, as the process of reading is extremely complex and does not lend itself to a rigid analysis of this sort.

Since many students who read braille attend classes alongside their peers who are sighted, suggestions for teachers of students with visual impairments for facilitating the generalization of braille reading skills into the general education classroom are offered.

Role of the Teacher of Students With Visual Impairments

The beginning braille reader will need direct instruction from a teacher of students with visual impairments to gain foundational braille literacy skills. According to a Delphi study conducted by Koenig and Holbrook (2000), for beginning braille readers (preK–Grade 3), "consistency (daily contact) by a teacher of students with visual impairments is essential to ensure the development of braille literacy," and, "one to two hours of instruction is needed daily" (p. 688). The teacher of students with visual impairments knows and understands braille, and is equipped to teach it. They also understand what method of instruction to implement based on each student's individual needs. It is imperative students receive daily intensive direct instruction by a teacher of students with visual impairments in order to develop fundamental braille literacy skills.

Attitude Development

A child's first impression of braille is extremely important. Various suggestions were made in Chapter 3 for fostering good attitudes and providing preschool exposure to braille. There is a definite need to continue this effort when the child starts school or begins actual braille instruction. The following activities are suggested for encouraging a positive attitude toward beginning instruction:

1. Label the child's school surroundings with contracted braille. This might include their desk, bookshelves, books, locker, brailler, miscellaneous school supplies, the teacher's desk, wastebasket, pencil sharpener, and bulletin board. Physically guide the child to the location of each label and read it to them.

2. Provide good models of braille reading. If the teacher is not a tactual braille reader, an outside resource person might be invited during "book sharing time." Children who are sighted will also benefit from this demonstration.

3. Demonstrate how braille is read by placing hands under the child's hands (hand-under-hand approach) as both hands are moved down a page. Discuss with the child examples of times braille might be used in everyday living.

4. Read to the child books that have both print and braille in them. Have the child "follow along" even though they are not decoding the braille in the beginning.

5. Have children dictate a few short sentences describing an experience that is important to them. Braille the sentences describing an experience that is important to them. Braille the sentences for them to "read" back. Braille songs, television commercials, or nursery rhymes the child has memorized can also be brailled.

6. Make the child's first braille books interesting for them to explore. Make the pages a different shape occasionally (e.g., round, triangular, tree-shaped, animal-shaped). The shape may actually give the child a "clue" as to what the book is about. The cover can be made tactually interesting by covering it with fabrics, small objects, string designs, etc. This could be made into an art project.

7. Create braille printed items that peers who are sighted would enjoy examining (e.g., calendars, lunch menus, special program agendas, and notes to parents.)

Do not place the beginning braille reader in a general education setting until they have the skills to "keep up" and feel successful. For the first several weeks of the school year, scheduled time outside of the general education (if the student is in a mainstream setting) may be required to give intensive instruction in braille reading. Before joining a reading group with print readers, beginning braille readers should also know how to locate stories using the table of contents and to locate page numbers.

Mechanical Skills

Outlined below are a number of mechanical skills unique to braille reading. These skills must be well developed before placing any emphasis on decoding braille words, phrases, or sentences.

Finger Dexterity and Wrist Flexibility

1. Involve the child in sorting and stacking activities. Begin with large, familiar objects and toys. Gradually introduce smaller objects such as nails and paper clips.

2. Provide beads for stringing, with the sizes becoming progressively smaller.

3. Give the child braille paper to punch. Have them "sew" with yarn through the punched holes. Additional art projects that encourage fine finger manipulations are paper weaving, paper folding, cutting, and pasting.

4. Collect various sizes of jars with screw caps. Have the child sort small objects and put them into the jars. Nuts and bolts of various sizes also provide similar kinds of movement.

5. Combine teaching of math concepts and counting with fine motor activities. One example is having the child attach pinch clothespins on a hanger for simple counting purposes. Each fine motor task should be accomplished with each hand separately as well as both hands together.

6. Record directions to some of the above activities so the child can practice working independently.

Hand Movements and Finger Positions

1. Demonstrate correct finger position for braille reading. Use a book or the edge of a ruler to help the child learn the correct curvature for their fingers.

2. Make some simulated reading materials to help teach hand movement. These simulated reading materials might consist of popsicle sticks or yarn glued to braille paper. Thread lines made with a sewing machine or lines of a single repeated braille symbol may also be used. The purpose of not using real braille reading material at this point is to remove the child's focus from the geometry of the braille symbols so they can concentrate on the more generalized skill of efficient hand movement and finger placement.

3. Introduce terminology that will help the child remember that each finger has a function. For example, there are "lead fingers" and "detectives."

Even though two or three fingers may take major responsibility for reading, all other fingers are needed for verification or "checking up" on these lead fingers. Children very quickly become comfortable using just a single finger; teachers must resist the temptation to allow this pattern. Although the student's short-range efficiency appears better with one hand, long-range efficiency will suffer if both hands are not used.

4. Demonstrate the smooth, independent movements of the hands to the student. The student's hands can be placed atop the educator's during this activity.

5. Make tracking activities pleasureable, meaningful, and authentic. Gayle Lamb (1996) supports the use of a whole language approach, whereby children learn to read and write in the same way they learn to speak and to listen (p. 184). The teaching strategy and activities below are direct quotes from her article (pp. 186–187). *The Three Billy Goat's Gruff* was used as the text for this activity.

    a. Text (read coactively): "The big billy goat went over the bridge to eat the grass."

    b. Patterns used to represent key elements:
    bridge   grass
    ⠿⠿⠿⠿⠿⠿⠿⠿⠿⠿⠿⠿⠿⠿⠿⠿⠿⠿⠿⠿⠿⠿⠿⠇⠇⠇⠇⠇⠇⠇⠇⠇⠇⠇⠇⠇⠇⠇⠇
                              troll

    c. Sample Activities:

        i. You be the billy goat and cross the bridge.

        ii. Tiptoe over the bridge, so the troll can't hear you [encourage left-right tracking and a light touch].

        iii. Can you get across the bridge without the troll catching you? Go quickly and lightly [encourages speed and a light touch].

        iv. Where's the troll? Can you find him? [develops the concept of the word and scanning skills].

        v. What does troll start with? Let's write the little "t." What other words do you know that start with "t"? [develops sound-symbol relations hips and early writing].

6. Described in Chapter 3, *The Mangold Braille Program* provides lessons that are carefully sequenced and based upon criteria for mastery. Mangold recommends tracking double-spaced lines of repeated braille characters as shown below to establish rapid, smooth hand movements. To assist a student moving from line to line, horizontal or vertical (tactual) line guides are suggested.

    Double Spaced c's with Vertical Line Guide for the Left Hand
    ⠇⠉ ⠉

Double Spaced c's with Vertical Midline Guide

Double Spaced g's with Diagonal Line Guide for Return Sweeps to Next Line

When smooth tracking is accomplished with a single hand, two-handed tracking is introduced with double-spaced two-columned braille. The student is directed to read across the line with both hands until they come to a vertical line. At this point, the left hand is to return to the beginning of the next line, while the right hand finishes the current line. The tactual vertical line separating the two columns of braille is later replaced by several blank spaces.

Children will develop their own best tracking patterns; thus, it is important to encourage experimentation with respect to how the left hand returns to the beginning of a new line or at what point the left hand begins its return. Some excellent braille readers go down to the new line at the halfway point on the current line and track backward over the new line to its beginning. Many of these readers report picking up some information as they do this "backward reading."

Below are examples to illustrate the exercises and recommended sequences, excerpted from the *Mangold Braille Program, Basic Braille Unit 1 & 2*.

Lesson 1 (Braille Page 17)

This exercise will teach a student how to use his hands independently. Some students are ready to use their hands independently as soon as they begin reading braille. Other students use both hands together for a long time before they can easily use their hands independently. If on page 17 the student becomes frustrated or begins to skip lines remove pages 17 through 22 and place them at the end of lesson 14 for later use.

Use the following instructions when you braille pages 17–22.

Direct the student to track across the short lines with both hands together or go over all of the lines on the left side of the page first, then the right side of the page. Now have the student go to the top of the page. Think about the two short lines as being one long line all the way across the page. Have the student track the left short line with both hands, stop at the vertical line, and finish tracking the right side with his right hand only. Do every line the same way. Allow the student to use this method on the criterion test if they choose.

Double Space Two Column Repetitious Braille Independent Hand Movements

Orientation to the Page

1. Illustrate what is meant by "margin" (top, bottom, left, right). Give the child practice tracking from one margin to another.
2. Teach the child about spacing and paragraphing by using repetitive braille in the format of real braille.
3. Have the child count the number of indented lines found while tracking rapidly down a page.

Light Finger Touch

1. Place checkers on braille graph paper and have the child practice touching them so lightly that they do not move outside of the square.
2. Have the child rub their fingers in colored chalk and then track across pages of old magazines to see how long they can track making continuous contact before they run out of color. Tell the student how well they

are progressing in this task. The student will feel more involved if they record and chart their progress.

3. Demonstrate how lightly braille should be touched. Have the child practice this light touch while giving them praise for making light continuous contact without "scrubbing" the dots.

4. Construct a homemade tachistoscope for the child. One way to do this is to braille repetitious symbols on paper tape. Pull the tape beneath the child's fingers as they place them over the edge of a book or a ruler. The purpose of this activity is to see how high they can hold their fingers and still detect the presence or absence of braille symbols. When ready to work on discrimination of the symbols, this exercise can be used again to pick out the symbol that is different.

Tactile Perception and Discrimination

Once the mechanical skills are mastered, children are ready to sharpen their tactile perception and recognize differences among braille configurations. There is no right way to introduce this phase of instruction. Some teachers introduce the braille alphabet first; others introduce whole words in the beginning. Most teachers, however, modify their approach according to the needs of individual children. Including some language experience stories as a part of every child's initial exposure to braille is important. After several readings of material the children have dictated, they begin to make associations between symbols and their meanings. The teacher may wish to control the vocabulary studied to avoid use of lower cell contractions—or even contractions of any kind.

For those teachers choosing to introduce alphabet letters first, it might help to make a list of words commonly used in a kindergarten or primary setting. For example, color words are often referred to at this level. Some of the color words—blue, orange, purple, black—contain no contractions and might be appropriate for a starting list. If the resource teacher or support person makes a tactual drawing within which the student who is visually impaired can color, these drawings can be labeled with the color words; the child's crayon should also be labeled. Large, triangular crayons work very well with children who are blind because they do not roll off desks easily and have a large enough surface to attach a label. For students who do not see colors well, it is important to provide additional context. For example, tell children strawberries are red; the sky is blue on a clear day; clouds are white; and even, black is not a good color to wear on a walk at night because drivers cannot see a person dressed in black well as there is no contrast between the dark clothing and the dark of the night.

Tactual drawings can be made several ways. A quick method for producing a tactual outline is on a screenboard. A screenboard can be made by attaching a piece of metal screening to the back of a flannel board; the edges should be bound with masking tape. When the student writes with crayon (the paper is placed on top of the screen), the lines can be easily detected tactually.

Regardless of the approach each teacher chooses when introducing meaning to braille symbols, care must be taken with respect to description and timing. Symbols that are reversible pairs ("i" and "e"; "r" and "w"; "of" and "with"; "er" and "q"; "ou" and "t"; "sh" and "m"; "u" and "ing") ought not to be introduced together; one of each pair needs to be mastered before the other is learned. Although it is helpful for children to know that the six dots in a braille cell are numbered, it is not important for children to recall the numbers every time the symbol is encountered. In other words, the student needs to learn the geometric shape of each braille cell without having to memorize the dot numbers composing each shape.

Dr. Sally Mangold developed and field tested a program for teaching tactile perception and braille letter recognition. Mangold found through her experience as a resource teacher that preschool children who are blind do not get the exposure to left-right tracking or to letter recognition that sighted children receive. Because her program is based upon a precision teaching model, it is described in some depth below.

Mangold Braille Program, Basic Braille Units 1 & 2

(originally The Mangold Developmental Program of Tactile Perception and Braille Letter Recognition)

Good Two-Handed Reading

Mangold conducted a study to determine the extent to which a developmental program of perception and recognition might decrease scrubbing, backtracking, and letter reversal errors of braille readers. The model program required 12 to 16 weeks to administer, depending upon the abilities of each of the 30 subjects (ages 5 to 15 years).

The sequenced exercises that make up this program are designed to teach the mechanics of braille reading—the characteristic hand positions and movement techniques typical of good two-handed braille readers. It is assumed that the task of decoding abstract symbols becomes easier if the reader has already mastered tracking, skimming, identification of like and different, light finger touch, and left-to-right movement of the hands.

The proponents of precision teaching believe that a student who overlearns a skill will incorporate it so thoroughly in their repertoire of knowledge that when they move on, they will not confuse items that are familiar with newly introduced material (e.g., "e" [⠑] and "i" [⠊] in braille. The student will also expend little energy performing an overlearned skill and will consequently have greater energy available to apply to mastery of the new skill.

Data analysis revealed that, as hypothesized, the experimental subjects demonstrated significantly fewer errors in tactile perception, braille letter recognition, and undesirable backtracking and scrubbing. This result was true of the subjects who were new braille readers, as well as of those who had a history of reading difficulties.

Precision teaching assessment techniques used throughout the study resulted in the establishment of criteria for 19 subskills of tactile perception and braille letter recognition. If a student can perform a particular task at the rate recommended, it is suggested that they skip worksheets teaching that skill and proceed to a higher level of difficulty. Practice worksheets are included after each criterion test for use by those students who have not yet mastered the skill under consideration.

Precision teaching is not a new teaching approach. It is designed to supplement an existing program and can be used by teachers who have a wide variety of teaching styles. It has four parts:

1. A skill to be mastered is identified.

2. The skill is broken down into subskills by the teacher.

3. The student is assessed by the teacher on these subskills to ascertain their current rate of response.

4. A daily one-minute timing on each skill designated by the teacher is done on three consecutive days to determine the student's potential rate of progress.

Following is an example of this precision approach. A student might be assessed on the ability to read and say a lower-case letter. The letters are presented in a horizontal format and written in a random order. The recommended mastery of this skill is 70 letters per minute. A student should improve at least 30 percent on a skill during a 10-day period. Many students will improve more than this. If a student falls below the 30 percent improvement level, it is probably because the skill being taught is too difficult. An easier task should be substituted for the current one.

The *Mangold Program* is not designed to be a complete program of reading instruction. It should be used for only that portion of reading instruction devoted to tactile perception and braille letter recognition. In most schools, this program would constitute about one-third of the reading period. Concept development, auditory discrimination, and phonetic skills are also vital elements in a comprehensive reading instruction program.

The decision as to the appropriateness of the developmental program for a particular student must be based on knowledge of the student's overall level of functioning, and their ability to comprehend language, attend to task, and manipulate objects. The purpose of the *Mangold Program* is not only to produce students who read well but to produce students who love to read.

The 29 lessons of the Mangold Basic Braille Program include criteria tests and worksheets that promote mastery of the following skills:

1. Tracking from left to right across like symbols that follow closely without a space between them.

2. Tracking from left to right across unlike symbols that follow closely without a space between them.
3. Tracking from left to right across like symbols that have one or two blank spaces between them.
4. Tracking from left to right across unlike symbols that have one or two blank spaces between them.
5. Tracking from top to bottom over like symbols that follow closely without a space between them.
6. Tracking from top to bottom over unlike symbols that follow closely without a space between them.
7. Tracking from top to bottom over like symbols that have one blank space between them.
8. Tracking from top to bottom over unlike symbols that have one blank space between them.
9. Identifying two geometric shapes as being the same or different.
10. Identifying two braille symbols as being the same or different.
11. Identifying two braille symbols as being the same or different when they are preceded and followed by a solid line.
12. Identifying the one symbol that is different within a line of like symbols using a variety of braille symbols for different lines.
13. Identifying the one symbol that is different within a group of three symbols, two of which are identical.

Lessons 15 through 29 introduce the letters of the alphabet in the following sequence: c, g, l, d, y, a, b, s, w, p, k, r, m, e, h, n, x, z, f, u, t, q, i, v, j.

Games using skills that have been mastered are scattered throughout the program. These games, along with suggested achievement charting, have proven to maintain a high level of student motivation. Exceptional Teaching Aids (exceptionalteaching.com/mangold-exclusivesincluding-mangold-braille-math/; 800-549-6999) can provide more information upon request.

Kinesthetic Skills

When teaching rapid reading to exceptional readers, it becomes essential to break bad mechanical habits. A technique for breaking these habits is reading for no comprehension. The value of this technique is to establish the *kinesthetic* or internal feeling of reading smoothly and rapidly. When applied to the teaching of beginning reading, it can involve much "pretend reading." The child should be given the opportunity to "read" material that is memorized before learning to decode braille symbols. This kind of activity should be scattered throughout the period during which discriminatory skills are developing as well. For some children, timing and charting the number of pages covered in 1 minute is a useful and motivating technique.

Ergonomics

Creating a workspace that supports the student in reading and writing braille efficiently is an important component of the reading process and is often overlooked. Good posture and position is necessary for the child to keep their fingers on the correct line and to maintain their place on the page. It also helps to reduce fatigue. Ensure the chair is set at a height where the child's feet are on the floor. The desk should be set at a height so the child's arms are parallel to the table when seated. A table is too high if the child's shoulders are near their ears.

Decoding Skills

In this section, decoding will be referred to in its narrowest sense—that of developing awareness of the sound-symbol relationship. While decoding of symbols cannot be completely isolated from comprehension, skills in decoding are nonetheless enhanced when the student uses context, structural clues, experiential background, sight vocabulary, and spelling patterns to understand the string of symbols being touched.

Some teachers approach decoding analytically. For instance, they have students note similarities among sight words such as "mother," "milk," and "man" when teaching the sound of "m." Other teachers prefer a synthetic approach that looks at sounds in isolation. These sounds are subsequently pronounced in rapid succession so that the student understands how words are built (blended). Regardless of the approach, the following suggestions may be helpful when working with braille readers:

1. Braille symbols that are reversible pairs should never be introduced together. Examples of reversal pairs include "e" [⠑] and "i" [⠊], "d" [⠙] and "f" [⠋], "h" [⠓] and "j" [⠚].

2. Short passages of the child's reading series can be recorded so that they are able to hear the sounds being pronounced, as their fingers pass over braille symbols. Bookshare is an e-book library for students with visual impairments and other disabilities that might affect their ability to access print materials. Students who utilize this library are able to listen to books, read in braille or large font, and follow along with highlighting. Bookshare (bookshare.org; 650-352-0198) is free for students who qualify.

3. When introducing or drilling sounds, objects that are familiar to the child should be substituted for picture-type stimuli. Below is a list of beginning-consonant, long-vowel, and short-vowel sounds with one or more objects to use for each:

Consonants	Long Vowels
b – ball	a – tape, cane
c – cup, cap, comb	e – peanut, leaf
d – doll, drum, dish	i – dime
f – feather, football, fan	o – go, toe, rope
g – gun, glasses, gum	u – ruler
h – horn, hook	
j – jack-in-the-box, jar, jump rope	Short Vowels
k – key, kite	a – can, apple
l – light bulb, lace	e – pen
m – mitten, magnet, match	i – pin
n – nail	o – top
p – paper, pencil, pen	u – sucker
q – quarter, quack (from rubber duck)	
r – rock, rubber band, ruler	
s – sucker, sock, sandpaper	

4. An independent activity for students is to match objects that have "like beginning sounds," "like ending sounds," or "like middle sounds."

5. Recording instructions to matching exercises fosters independence. In addition to matching objects, as in Item 3 above, the student may be asked to match brailled words to objects or brailled words to each other.

6. When asking students to do matching exercises, provide compartments for them to pair or group items. Muffin tins work very well if the items are small. For larger objects, several trays can be placed together.

7. As the student encounters symbols for the words they already know and use as part of their listening and speaking vocabulary, they are learning to associate a particular symbol with a known word. The student may notice that when they say a particular word, it is tactually a "short" one. The teacher can facilitate this use of configuration clues by pointing out the shape of braille words that the child encounters. For the beginning braille reader, the use of uncontracted words may be best because the length of the word will then be more directly related to the length of its sound.

8. Like peers who are sighted, braille readers require daily drill and practice in decoding. It is good to keep a record of students' errors each day, so that they have a better idea of readiness to advance.

Memorization of Braille Code Rules

Individuals who learn the braille code by sight must memorize the rules for using it. Fortunately, children who are blind learn these rules incidentally as they read braille. Although teachers may wish to discuss a particular rule when the child is writing braille, there is little need to dwell on rules when teaching braille reading.

Vocabulary Development

During the primary grades, major attention is given to developing a sight vocabulary and the word-analysis skills that promote independent reading. The third-grade level reader shows a greater concern for developing the meaning of words, transitioning away from emphasizing decoding "new" words. From then on, one of the major objectives of reading instruction is helping children to build reading vocabularies that are wide ranging, rich, and accurate.

Below are several ideas to enhance vocabulary development with accompanying adaptions for the braille reader.

1. Writing experience stories is a good way to promote vocabulary development. Words that have been confined to the child's listening vocabulary may be transferred to their speaking vocabulary and ultimately to their reading vocabulary. The major advantage of using experience stories is that they are motivating. Students see words that are meaningful to them because they describe their own experiences. For the child who has not mastered decoding skills, it is still possible to read through reliance on memory. The major disadvantage of using experience stories is that there is no control over vocabulary used. We know that some contractions are more difficult to recognize than others (i.e., lower cell contractions, two cell contractions). To overcome this problem, the teacher must guide the selection of words for experience stories. This is done by suggesting experiences to write about and by phrasing questions in a way that elicits specific vocabulary words. In addition to choosing words that are easier to recognize tactually, the teacher must be aware of words that children are encountering in their classroom reading series; these words can be practiced during the time spent with the resource or itinerant teacher.

2. The teacher of students with visual impairments can supplement the classroom teacher's vocabulary-building efforts by taking note of the pictures that the basal reading series contains. If at all feasible, the child who is visually impaired should be given the opportunity to "experience" the activities portrayed in these pictures. This strategy may involve giving the information to the child's parents through a phone call, meeting, or letter.

3. Verify that children who are blind understand the meaning of words. Ask children to demonstrate their understanding through body gestures.

4. Help students categorize words. Begin with having the child identify names or action words. Additional categories might be animals, food, clothing items, etc. If the words are brailled on flash cards, they can be placed into sectioned boxes, tied or clipped to a string, or pinned on a line. Regular classroom teachers may develop category games in which the child spins a dial and has to name a word fitting the category indicated when the dial stops. The teacher of students with visual impairments can facilitate participation of the child who is visually impaired when the dial stops. The teacher can also facilitate the student's participation in such games by brailling labels for the gameboard or the cards used.

5. Present new words to students in context, rather than in isolation. Have students construct their own notebook or dictionary of new words. Instead of writing a definition of the word, a sentence might be written beside the word, illustrating its meaning through context.

6. When transcribing story books to braille, vary the shape of the pages and the cover. Children who are sighted are attracted to a book largely by attractive and interesting book jackets. Children who are braille readers cannot be expected to be enthusiastic about identical rectangular sheets of braille paper.

7. To further develop vocabulary, the regular classroom teacher may use rhyming exercises and the study of roots, prefixes, and suffixes. Most of these exercises will require the teacher of students with visual impairments to transcribe print to braille or provide recorded exercises. The format of some of the print materials may also need to be changed. Guidelines for these format changes are discussed in depth at the end of the chapter.

Comprehension Skills

The development of adequate comprehension skills is a very complex process. Students must not only be able to understand what the author is saying, *literal comprehension*, but must also be able to infer meaning, *inferential comprehension*, and make judgment about what is read, *evaluation comprehension*. It is also important for students to enjoy and appreciate the literary qualities of a story.

Comprehension skills can be taught in numerous ways. Regardless of the approach used, it is at first essential for reading material to be kept interesting and brief. Specific ideas are as follows:

1. When working on comprehension skills, allow the student to read in a quiet area, apart from a group. Gradually build tolerance for noise and distraction so that the student can function independently in a classroom with several children.

2. As with vocabulary building, the student needs first-hand experiences in order to relate to the braille words on a page. Many concepts can be developed through exposure to real objects that the student can handle.

3. When children who are blind are reading, encourage them to use tactual, auditory, and kinesthetic imagery. Ask children questions about what they smell, feel, and taste while reading a particular story. If students have previously been sighted, they may also be able to conjure up visual images of things described in the reading. When first working on this skill, have students listen to books in audio formats, so that their progress can be monitored. Stop the recording occasionally and discuss what a word, phrase, or sentence causes the student to see, taste, hear, or feel.

4. Configuration or shape clues were discussed under decoding skills earlier in this chapter. Encourage students to use this technique when reading for comprehension as well. One way to begin working on this skill is to develop an automatic vocabulary of sight words, since a relatively small number of words make up a high proportion of most reading material. The Dolch Word List is a commercially available list of sight words. These may be brailled on flash cards and used for drill. Another useful tool is *All Aboard! The Sight Word Activity Express* from the American Printing House for the Blind (APH), which helps with instruction and assessment of a student's recognition of high frequency words. In addition to commonly appearing words, frequently occurring letter combinations might also be studied for their unique shapes.

5. Closely related to the use of shape clues to enhance comprehension skills is the use of structural clues. The teacher of students with visual impairments must point out word beginnings, endings, spelling patterns, and letter repetitions, which will give additional clues to the reader. By brailling sentences with missing letters, word parts, and words, the teacher can illustrate the use of structural clues.

6. Brailled exercises with deleted words and phrases can be used to practice the use of context clues. Another activity that encourages the use of context is scanning a page rapidly to pick up two or three words. Further rereadings of the same page helps to fill in missing details and provides more practice in using context clues.

7. Make frequent checks of comprehension. Do not rely on "factual" questions, but ask how children feel about what they have read. For example: "What happened in the story that happened to you?"; "How did you feel when you read about _____?"; and "How would you change this story to make it better?" (See Appendix A for further illustrations of nonfactual questions).

8. Children who are sighted rely heavily on pictures for understanding printed words on a page. Children who are blind can gain some of this type of information during silent reading periods by listening to recorded descriptions of the pictures in a particular story.

9. Give braille readers opportunities to read a variety of material. As readers progress through school, they need to be exposed to poetry, fiction, descriptive material, editorials, and directions, such as recipes.

Flexibility Skills

While it is essential that children read smoothly and fluently, it is even more important for them to be flexible readers. They should be able to vary their reading speed according to the material encountered and the reasons for reading that material. Teachers must therefore deliberately introduce reading activities with some direction for *how* the children should be reading. This implies giving readers a variety of materials on which to practice and giving them specific purposes for reading. The following are suggestions for teaching scanning, skimming, and reflective reading.

Scan Reading

The purpose of "scan reading" is to locate a specific item or items on a page without attempting to understand the context in which they appear. Tables of contents, indexes, telephone directories, and dictionaries are good materials for practicing this skill. Although it is not practical to think in terms of a braille telephone directory, it is realistic to think that a braille reader may have a page or two of telephone numbers to scan. Columns of numbers can be used as exercises in "looking at" numbers. Children often enjoy making a time game of scanning; this may even extend to having them take open book examinations. Before beginning the search for an item on a page, children should be told to imagine how that item will *feel* under their fingers when they locate it. Expecting the item to stand out tactually facilitates scan reading.

Skim Reading

The reason one *skim reads* is to get an overview of something. It implies putting bits and pieces together to get the whole picture. Tables of contents, introductions, titles, subtitles, summaries, and topic sentences of individual paragraphs are appropriate for teaching skimming. Here are more specific techniques for introducing this type of reading:

1. When administering a reading assignment, give the student general questions to answer. Have the student practice formulating questions based on book titles, chapter headings, etc.

2. Identify and drill for rapid recognition of *sign-post* words that signal a continuation of thought. Examples of sign-post words are "and," "also," "likewise," "moreover," and "furthermore." Additionally, identify and drill for rapid recognition of *turn-about* words that change the direction of

thought. Examples of words like this are "but," "yet," "nevertheless," and "despite." The beginning reader may not encounter some of these examples; the teacher should drill those which are appropriate to the material the child is reading.

3. As previously mentioned under the development of comprehension skills, have the child practice rapid, automatic recognition of common words. A list such as the Dolch words should be brailled on flash cards and in vertical and horizontal lists.

4. Set rate and comprehension goals for material that is being read. Have children time and challenge themselves regularly. The timing procedure can be made an independent activity if students are allowed to use technology (such as stopwatch features) on their personal technology devices. For a low-tech option, use a device to record "go" and "stop" at 30-second or 60-second intervals.

5. As with scan reading, open book examinations will facilitate the practice of reading for main ideas.

6. Reinforce reading for the main idea through writing activities. Discuss logical organization and sequencing of ideas initially. Follow this discussion with the directions to write sample paragraphs that are easy versus hard to skim for the main idea.

7. A good skimming technique was described under the development of comprehension skills. It was suggested that students gain practice in using context clues by rapidly rereading a single page several times. This technique might be called *bits-and-pieces reading* because initially the student is asked to pick out only two or three words per page. As children reread the same page, they pick up additional words to fill in missing details.

Reading Style Development

How children sit (or stand), hold a book, and move their hands determines their *braille reading style*. A broader definition of reading style might also include desire for quiet or ambient noise, presence or absence of subvocalization, or body movements while reading. In Chapter 2, some reading styles are mentioned that appear to be preferable, in that most "good" braille readers use them. Nevertheless, the important thing to keep in mind is that reading style is highly individual, and children must be encouraged to experiment to determine what reading style best suits them. Listed below are some ways teachers can foster this experimentation:

1. Provide a variety of reading environments by (a) varying the noise level; (b) introducing chair and table combinations that differ in height; (c) allowing children to sit on floor cushions occasionally for reading.

2. Demonstrate ways to hold a braille book: parallel versus at a slight angle, using a book prop or slant board, using one's lap.
3. Demonstrate ways to move one's hands independently across a braille page. Help the student experiment with innovative ways of moving their hands.
4. Help the child reduce subvocalizations by placing a pencil between the child's teeth while reading and having the student suck on hard candy while reading.
5. Encourage children to discuss their braille reading styles with each other.

Carryover Skills: Special Setting to the General Education Classroom

Most of the suggestions given for the aforementioned skill areas were geared toward the teacher of students with visual impairments. Nonetheless, the teacher in the general education setting also must be familiar with work the child does outside their classroom. Furthermore, knowledge of the role of the teacher of students with visual impairments helps the general education classroom teacher cooperate more effectively, and thus provide better carryover. Following are a few ways in which all teachers working with braille readers contribute to the team effort and enhance the braille reader's educational experience.

General Education Teacher

General classroom teachers need to plan ahead with respect to skill objectives and materials. By outlining the objectives of their reading programs and giving the teacher of students with visual impairments a list of texts, worksheets, and tests ahead of time, the general classroom teacher helps the braille-reading child keep up with their peers who are sighted. This kind of cooperation gives the teacher of students with visual impairments time to transcribe or create materials and enables them to do supplementary tutoring in the skill areas when needed. These teachers will have to decide how much "lead time" is needed for transcribing, ordering books or equipment, and creating tactile graphics, etc. A great deal will depend on the availability of a transcriber or paraeducator who is proficient in braille. A teacher of students with visual impairments working alone cannot be expected to accomplish these tasks in a few short days. As soon as the classroom placement of a child who is visually impaired is known, the teacher of children with visual impairments and the general education classroom teacher should meet to discuss materials needed for the upcoming school year.

Resource or Itinerant Teacher

Establishing a good relationship with the general education teacher during the spring preceding the fall entry to school of the child who is visually impaired is helpful. It is vitally important for the teacher of students with visual impairments to be familiar with the reading curriculum and routine used in the general education classroom. When general education teachers feel comfortable with the teacher of students with visual impairments as a person, they are more likely to allow observations of their classroom without fear of being critically judged. A regular system of communication must be established between these teachers. This might mean setting up a particular day of the week or time of the day for collaborating together. When this is impossible, it may involve agreeing upon a place for picking up and delivering transcribed material. Following are a few suggestions for the resource or itinerant teacher that will help facilitate the use of braille in the general education classroom.

1. The following materials should be available to the general education teacher at the beginning of the year:

    - braille versions of the first books to be used
    - braille versions of the first workbook pages to be used
    - braille wordlists or flashcards of vocabulary being introduced to the readers

    Note. Interline the flash cards with print so that children who are sighted can read them. Clip one corner of each flash card so that the student can tell which side is the front.

    - braille versions of school bulletins, menus, calendars (ongoing)
    - pushpin board with pushpins, approximately 11-by-11-inch cork or foam board covered with contact paper, (see Number 5 below for uses)
    - nonslip pad for placement of worksheets and for quieting the braillewriter's sound

2. Double-space all material that is transcribed from the first reader; double-space all worksheets that require a braille response on them. There is as much as a half-line discrepancy among braillewriters; double-spacing the worksheets allows the child to roll them into the braillewriter to record an answer without writing over something else.

3. Transcribe material having picture content according to the reason for inclusion of the picture.

    - If the picture does not enhance the meaning of the text and it is in fact unnecessary, omit reference to it.
    - If the picture consists of simple, familiar objects, a tracing wheel replica can be made. It is also possible to duplicate outlines in yarn, string, or electrician's narrow tape; these outlines may or may not be thermoformed, depending on the need for durability.

- If complex figures are used in print but are not needed for conveying the concept, substitute simple geometric shapes and braille characters, as shown.
    - Choose the ones that are different:

    Print Version:

    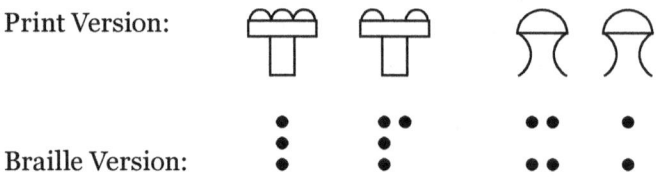

    Braille Version:

- If the picture enhances the content of the text, record a description of the picture.
- If the image demands understanding of detailed pictorial content, use objects or models supplemented by individual tutoring. Examples include:
    - Learn the exact location of a body part.
    - Interpret differences in two objects.
- If the picture is meant to arouse interest in a story or give a mere clue to its content, make a tactual substitution for the picture.
    - Feather = story about a duck or bird
    - Shoelace = story about shoes

4. When transcribing print materials to braille, it is often necessary to alter the format for ease of reading in braille as detailed below. BANA also offers *Guidelines for the Transcription of Early Educational Materials from Print to Braille* (2020) (brailleauthority.org/early_learning/index.html).

    - Directions for completing a worksheet should always appear at the top of a braille page, regardless of where they are found in print because braille versions of single-print pages may be two to three pages in length, and the directions may fall on the second or third page, causing confusion to the braille reader.
    - Dots 4–6, dots 3–6 [⠸ ⠤] are used in braille to indicate a blank for insertion of a braille answer. The student should be instructed to braille their answer after the blank, instead of above it, as is usually seen in print. This practice reduces the need to continuously roll the braille paper up or down to read and respond to the questions. Two spaces more than those needed for the correct answer should be provided to the right of the blank.

- On phonics exercises that give pictures as clues to decoding a choice of words, the stimulus word for the picture should be spoken or recorded. The child can choose the brailled word on the basis of the auditory stimulus.
5. A pushpin board and pushpins may be used to respond to a braille worksheet; the student puts a pinhole next to the chosen items or answers. The responses chosen from the pushpin worksheet should then be interlined with print by the teachers of students with visual impairments for the classroom teacher to read.
6. Print materials that are recorded must include pauses. A minimum of three seconds between directions and between individual questions should be left on the recording made for a braille student. This time lag allows the student to turn the recording off before brailling a response and to turn it back on to listen to the next item.
7. When transcribing programmed material for the braille reader, the direction of the binding may have to be changed. The textual materials and questions can be bound on the left, just as print materials are bound. The self-checking key, however, is best used by the braille reader if it is bound on the right. The transcriber should make certain that the spacing of the questions matches the spacing of the answers.
8. Transcribed materials should be used for supplementary tutoring whenever feasible. Materials brailled for the teacher in the general education classroom can often be used by the teachers of students with visual impairments for multiple purposes in a tutoring session. Below are some examples:
    - Put a pushpin in all the words beginning with the sound of "m."
    - Put a pushpin in all the words that rhyme with "cat."
    - Braille a list of all the words that name things to wear.
    - Count the number of [insert symbol child confuses] on this page.

References

Bammen, H., Dawson, N., & McGovern, J. (1973). *Fundamentals of basic reading instruction*. New York, NY: McKay.

Braille Authority of North America (2020). *BANA Guidelines for the transcription of early educational materials from print to braille*. http://brailleauthority.org/early_learning/index.html

Bloom, B. (1974). Time and learning. *American Psychologist. 29*(9), 682–688.

Douglas, S., & Mangold, S. (1975). Precision teaching of visually impaired students. *Education of the Visually Handicapped. 7*(2), 48–52.

Grunwald, A. (1967). A braille-reading machine. *Science.* https://doi.org/10.1126/science.154.3745.144

Harris, A., & Sipay, E. (1971). *Effective teaching of reading.* New York, NY: McKay.

Heber, R. (1967). *A study of programmed instruction in braille* (ED015303). ERIC. https://eric.ed.gov/?q=ED015303&id=ED015303

Kederis, C. (1971). *Training for increasing braille reading rates* (ED023229). ERIC. https://eric.ed.gov/?id=ED023229

Lamb, G. (1996). Beginning braille: A whole language-based strategy. *Journal of Visual Impairment and Blindness. 90*(3), 184–189.

Mangold, S. (1977). *The Mangold developmental program of tactile perception and braille letter recognition.* Exceptional Teaching Aids.

Mangold, S. (1977). *The effects of a developmental teaching approach on tactile perception and braille letter recognition based on a model of precision teaching.* San Francisco: California State University.

Mangold, S. (1978). Tactile perception and braille letter recognition: Effects of developmental teaching. *Journal of Visual Impairment and Blindness. 72*(7), 259–266.

McBride, V. (1974). Explorations in rapid reading of braille. *New Outlook for the Blind,* 68, 8–13.

Olson, M. (1975). *The effects of training in rapid reading on the reading rate and comprehension of braille and large print readers.* University Microfilms.

Spache, G. (1972). *The teaching of reading.* Phi Delta Kappa.

Umsted, R. (1970). *Improvement of braille reading through code recognition and training.* University Microfilms.

Wallace, D. (1973). *The effect of rapid reading instruction and recognition training on the reading rate and comprehension of adult legally blind print and braille readers.* [Unpublished doctoral dissertation]. Brigham Young University.

CHAPTER 5

Ideas for Working With Striving Readers

Striving Readers of Braille

A *striving reader* generally falls into one of two categories: The student has either not learned to read in any other medium than braille or is a former reader of print. This scenario does not imply that having once been a reader of print makes a child a striving reader of braille. If these students have difficulty with braille, they usually have had difficulty with print also. They will be considered a separate remedial group in this book because their difficulties often need to be handled in a different way from those of children who have not been exposed to print.

Fourteen general areas of remediation will be first outlined and then discussed in this chapter. These remediation areas apply no matter what the reader's background. Teachers may find that many students function highly in all but one or two areas and that altering their teaching approach is all that is needed. For example, the student who is poor in auditory discrimination, and thus phonetic analysis, may not need remediation if the teacher presents the reading program by sight words and contextual reading. After the discussion of general remedial areas, the factors unique to former readers of print are presented.

General Areas of Remediation

For ease of discussion, the difficulties of remedial readers of braille have been categorized into 14 general areas. For a more complete assessment checklist, see Appendix A.

1. Book Handling and Posture
2. Locating Skills—book sections, page numbers, paragraphs, lines
3. Finger Curvature and Hand Relaxation
4. Lightness of Touch
5. Hand Movements—smoothness, continuity, independence
6. Symbol Recognition—letters, words, punctuation, numbers
7. Phonetic Analysis
8. Structural Analysis
9. Contextual Reading
10. Comprehension—literal, interpretative, critical thinking and problem solving

11. Rate of Reading
12. Flexibility of Reading Rate—type of material, purpose for reading
13. Oral Expression
14. Attitude and Motivation

Remediation Techniques

The remediation techniques discussed in this section are not comprehensive, but rather are intended as a few beginning guidelines. They may pertain to any striving reader, but teachers will need to tailor them to fit individual students and may expand upon them according to program resources. Many of the readiness or beginning reading activities suggested in Chapters 3 and 4 can be used with striving readers, although the focus of this section is on techniques that are an extension of other such activities.

The appropriateness of any one technique will depend largely upon the student's previous reading program. In some cases, the student requiring remediation has learned from a single teacher. More often than not, the student has been introduced to braille by someone other than the teacher providing remediation. It is therefore essential that a thorough assessment of each student's braille reading skills be completed before beginning any program of remediation.

Book Handling and Posture

The reader who tires quickly or is reading inefficiently because of awkward book handling must be given an opportunity to experiment with sitting postures and book position. The teacher might check the student's reading rate for each position tried. If the student's body is tense, no reading posture will be efficient. It may be necessary to have the student lie on their back and listen to music to relax before beginning to read. A small vibrating toy used across the shoulder area also helps relieve muscle tension before braille reading. Once one or more postures have been identified as more comfortable and efficient, the student must commit to practice times throughout the day.

Locating Skills

The student who is unable to locate parts of a book or lines on a page may need to focus on the basic concepts of top, bottom, right, left, beginning, and end. (For a detailed discussion of how this may be accomplished, see the section "Concept Development" in Chapter 3.) The teacher may also make a time game of locating page numbers, paragraphs, and section headings. By disassembling old braille books, several worksheets can be prepared for the student to work on independently. Direct the student to locate various items on a page by asking them to place pushpins into the cork board to which the worksheet is attached, or use the *Tactile Editing Marks Kit* from American Printing House for the Blind (APH). If the directions are recorded, this activity can be carried out independently.

Finger Curvature and Hand Relaxation

For the student who is tracking braille with their fingers in a flat, outstretched position, a book or rolled towel can be placed beneath the lines of braille to force the fingers into a curved position. The thickness of the object should vary according to the length of the student's fingers from fingertip to knuckle. This ergonomic position will reinforce proper finger placement.

If the student's hands seem tense or stiff, a warm-up relaxation period may be required at the beginning of each reading period. An exercise that is often helpful for relieving tension, as well as for strengthening muscles, is palm squeezing of stress balls, squishy fidgets, or soft modeling clay. The student might also shake their fingers loosely in the air or roll objects with their palm against a table surface. If a student has cold hands, perhaps from poor circulation, a small hair dryer or warm water can be used for a quick warmup.

Lightness of Touch

If a student's body is tense, they are likely to press too hard when reading braille; therefore, it is important to help the student relax their entire body. Tracking exercises for no comprehension may also prove necessary. If the teacher has not already used the activities suggested in Chapter 4, they may prove effective with the remedial reader of braille.

Hand Movements

Students who scrub braille, backtrack over lines previously read, or use only one hand when they have the potential to use two, will benefit from a program such as the *Mangold Braille Program, Basic Braille Unit 1 & 2*. As discussed in Chapter 4, part of this program is devoted to teaching smooth, continuous tracking patterns. Rate and performance criteria are built into carefully sequenced lessons. The teacher may also use language experience stories and memorized material to continue working on hand movements. Students are often surprised to realize that they absorb very little information during backtracking (rereading) movements; regressive hand movements most often become merely inefficient habits. The teacher might begin to prove this to students by having them read two stories that are comparable in difficulty level and length. For one passage, the student is directed to read in any manner they choose (backtracking included). For reading the second passage, restrict the student to continuous reading with no backtracking allowed. By comparing the percent comprehension achieved on the two passages the student should be able to see the relative inefficiency of backtracking movements.

Symbol Recognition

If the student consistently makes errors in the decoding process, observe first to see how they position their fingers with respect to the braille symbols. Braille characters are often misread because of inadequate fingertip coverage of the characters and the angle at which the hands are held. The student may be missing dots and thus misinterpreting individual symbols.

If the student's finger and hand positions are satisfactory, the teacher must next examine the type of decoding error being made. Using an enlarged braille cell to teach letters may increase the learning curve for beginning readers of braille (Barlow-Brown et al., 2018). Using an interactive cell, such as a swing cell, pegs and pegboard, or tennis balls in a muffin tin, may facilitate braille recognition at an earlier age.

If a student is confusing symbols that are reversible pairs—o/ow, e/I, d/f, h/j, r/w, m/sh, p/th, z/the, n/ed, st/ch, with/of, y/and, u/ing—or rotations of one another—s/wh, t/ou, ar/gh, ed/the, m/u, s/gh, er/with—one symbol of each pair needs to be overlearned before work begins on the other. Let us suppose that the student is confusing the letter "e" with the letter "i." They should be given exercises that have "e"'s mixed with other symbols in words and sentences. The only task would be to track the lines rapidly and verbally identify the "e"'s. When this task is accomplished with 100 percent accuracy and at an approximate rate of 80 verbalized "e"'s per minute, the symbol is considered "overlearned." The next step in remediation is then to begin a similar drill on the letter "i." Once the "i" is also overlearned, the two symbols can be mixed in words and sentences for discrimination. Giving students helpful hints for remembering specific symbols is also useful. For example, in discriminating between the braille symbol for numeral 5 and for numeral 9, the hint might be a saying: "The dots slant *up* for 9 because 9 is *higher* than 5." Additional ideas for overlearning symbol configurations can be found in Appendix B.

If the student is under 10 years old and making errors in identifying single letter contractions, a combination of braille phonics exercises and recordings is often effective. *Word PlayHouse* (APH) contains braille and print tiles on a felt board to make words and teach phonics and reading skills. *Lego Braille Bricks* is another APH product that can be used to teach braille through play. The *Mangold Basic Braille Program* is an additional resource for remediating braille letter recognition.

When the student excludes words during oral reading, the teacher needs to check the ensuing comprehension level. If excluding words does not distort the meaning of the passage for the student, the teacher should not be concerned with remediation in this area. If, however, the meaning is altered, one technique to try involves reading to the student. As the student follows along on the braille line being read, the teacher should periodically ask the student to fill in words whenever the teacher makes a deliberate pause.

Often a student consistently misses only particular words during oral reading. Should this happen, the teacher may again read aloud to the student at a rate close to the student's own reading rate. The teacher should read the troublesome words more loudly than the other words on the page. Once the teacher has modeled this procedure several times, the student should take the teacher's role in reading aloud and emphasizing the troublesome words.

An additional exercise is to provide the student with braille worksheets. On some of the worksheets, sentences are written with troublesome words replaced by blanks. Other worksheets might consist of complete sentences containing the particular words the student is missing. During these exercises, the student might be given points for each troublesome word identified. The teacher, on the other hand, would receive points for those remaining unidentified. If it seems suitable, the teacher may use a timer to introduce time limits to the student's search. Note that each of these exercises not only raises the student's level of awareness concerning the words they commonly miss, but also introduces extra drill on these words.

Phonetic Analysis

When a student is unable to decode words by phonetically breaking them down, the teacher must ask two basic questions. Firstly, is the student able to hear the difference among various phonemes? Many students have basic auditory processing difficulties; decoding words by phonetic analysis is simply impractical for these students, and the teacher must adjust their lessons to use a different approach for decoding words. Secondly, does the student listen to the differences between sounds? The teacher should decide if the student requires training in basic auditory discrimination or listening skills. Assuming the student has had a recent hearing evaluation, a high-frequency hearing loss can be eliminated. Individuals with high-frequency hearing losses often do not hear certain phonemes; they are prone to guess at the sounds from the faulty auditory input they have been receiving. Consultation with a speech-language pathologist or reading specialist is recommended when determining the best remediation techniques if students are unable to hear the difference among various phonemes or if auditory processing is suspected.

Once the teacher has established that a student can use phonetic analysis for decoding, the teacher can proceed with specific remedial techniques for improving the skill. One method that has been used successfully by many speech-language pathologists is that of kinesthetic-tactual sound reproduction. The student touches the teacher's throat or mouth while they are making a particular sound. The next step involves the student attempting similar throat and mouth movements while producing the same sound. The teacher should provide constant feedback to the child with repeated sessions of modeling. The student is asked to concentrate on the kinesthetic or internal feeling of sound production, and they correctly approximate the sound. This approach is supplemented by the teacher's verbal explanations of how a particular sound is produced (e.g., tightness of vocal cords, amount of air expulsion, position of the tongue).

Phonetic analysis often becomes easier for students when they use it in conjunction with contextual clues, word configuration, and structural analysis. Many basic phonic rules are learned incidentally in this manner. Chall's model of reading development explains that automatic decoding happens best when reading familiar words and patterns. Special attention should be given to texts that reinforce braille contractions that are currently being taught and already known. Simple, repetitive text helps students concentrate on word sounds instead of decoding unfamiliar words (Steinman et al., 2006).

Rhyming exercises have been used successfully by many teachers. Through these exercises, the student may work on words that begin or end with the same consonant, words that contain the same short or long vowel sounds, words that contain the same blends, or words that contain the same digraphs. Blends and digraphs that form braille contractions should always be presented to the student in their contracted form.

On occasion, a student is helped if a few basic phonic generalizations are drilled and memorized. One must not forget that phonetic analysis is a complex process. A single phoneme such as long "a" has eight possible sounds, depending upon what precedes or follows it (Bamman et al., 1973). Clymer (1963) conducted a study on the utility of 45 commonly taught phonic generalizations. Using an arbitrary criterion of 75 percent utility, he determined that only 18 phonic generalizations were stated specifically enough to aid a student in pronunciation of words contained in the basic reading series that introduced the generalizations. The remaining 28 generalizations had too many exceptions to be useful 75 percent of the time. Below is the list of 18 that *did* meet criterion:

1. The "r" gives the preceding vowel a sound that is neither long nor short.
2. Words having double "e" usually have the long "e" sound.
3. In "ay" the "y" is silent and gives "a" its long sound.
4. When "y" is the final letter in a word, it usually has a vowel sound.
5. When "c" and "h" are next to each other, they make only one sound.
6. "Ch" is usually pronounced as it is in "kitchen," "catch," and "chair," not like "sh."
7. When "c" is followed by "e" or "i," the sound of "s" is likely to be heard.
8. When the letter "c" is followed by "o" or "a," the sound of "k" is likely to be heard.
9. When "ght" is seen in a word, "gh" is silent.
10. When two of the same consonants are side by side, only one is heard.
11. When a word ends in "ck," it has the same last sound as in "look."
12. In most two-syllable words, the first syllable is accented.
13. If "a," "in," "re," "ex," "de" or "be" is the first syllable in a word, it is usually unaccented.
14. In most two-syllable words that end in a consonant followed by "y," the first syllable is accented and the last is unaccented.
15. If the last syllable of a word ends in "le," the consonant preceding the "le" usually begins the last syllable.

16. When the first vowel element in a word is followed by "th," "ch," or "sh," these symbols are not broken when the word is divided into syllables and may go with either the first or second syllable.
17. When there is one "e" in a word that ends in a consonant, the "e" usually has a short sound.
18. When the last syllable is the sound "r," it is unaccented.

If the teacher determines that a particular student might benefit from overlearning the previously described generalizations, the teacher might braille them on individual index cards with examples. To further practice their use, these generalizations may be used in a game situation in which the student is asked to give an example of the phonic rule that has been "spun" on a gameboard.

The regular classroom teacher may have any number of print games for reinforcing phonics skills. The vision teacher may find that some of them are adaptable for use by students of braille simply by transcribing print directions and labels to braille and adding tactual objects to substitute for pictures. A few commercial games that are highly recommended are described below.

1. *Speech to Print Phonics*: This game is structured for group work through the use of pupil response cards. It includes work on auditory discrimination, letter names, letter sounds, letter combinations, and applications of these skills to word attack situations. In addition to stressing sounds, context and meaning receive attention.
2. *Phonics We Use Learning Games*: This series is older, but copies can be found online. The games are attractive to children and require minimal teacher supervision. Included in this material are reinforcement exercises for learning the various consonant and vowel sounds and sound combinations.
3. *Consonant Lotto* and *Vowel Lotto:* These two games, utilizing Dolch words, are most beneficial after the sounds have been taught.

Structural Analysis
Morphology is the study of words and their parts. The smallest parts or units that have meaning are called morphemes (base words, prefixes, suffixes). Children who understand the structure of words can break them down into the smallest parts to gain meaning. They can also use those parts to change the meaning of words. These skills are important for building vocabulary. Students having difficulty in structural analysis of words usually find suffixes the most troublesome (Wilson, 1972). Results of the ABC Braille Study indicated that children were falling behind in vocabulary development by third grade. Compound words, though initially difficult to recognize, are easily broken into their component parts. When students

do not recognize the part, a sight word approach may be helpful. Because prefixes come at the beginning of words and have a definite effect on their meanings, they are easier to learn than suffixes. Most suffixes, when removed from their base words, leave these words with distorted configurations and spellings.

The teacher should consult any basal reading series for suggestions on remediating errors in structural analysis. Additionally, try the discovery approach to the study of specific prefixes, suffixes, and compound words. Whenever these word parts form braille contractions, as in the example for teaching the prefix "dis-" below, the teacher should present that word part in its contracted form.

1. Present a base word in a sentence: I like school.
2. Change the base word by adding the prefix: I dislike school.
3. Have the student generalize the difference in meaning between the first and second sentences.
4. Present several more words in a similar manner: agree/disagree; appear/disappear; comfort/discomfort; connect/disconnect; honest/dishonest.
5. Help the student generalize by asking what "dis-" does to the meaning of a base word.
6. From a dictionary, examine several words that begin with "dis-" and discuss with the student if they fit the generalization.
7. During contextual reading, continue to point out the prefix to the student. Again, reinforce its effect on base words.

Whenever the study of prefixes, suffixes, or compound words can be accomplished through games, the teacher must adapt such games for the braille student. Brailled game parts should then be interlined with print so that sighted classmates can read them. Several well-developed games for reinforcement of instruction in structural analysis can be purchased online. They are generally interesting to the student and have the additional advantage of peer group learning.

Contextual Reading
Students who fail to use the relationship of words within phrases, sentences, and paragraphs often have inadequate experiential backgrounds. Even if they were able to use contextual clues, they may not understand much of the vocabulary. When this is the case, the remedial teacher needs to alert the student's regular classroom teacher and parents or primary caregivers. They will need to provide as many "hands-on," direct experiences as possible.

Even when the student's experiential background is adequate, they may still not understand the function of context clues. Furthermore, when a student recognizes context clues once they are identified, they may not be able to anticipate them. Remediation of these difficulties requires much direct instruction and practice on a variety of literary styles.

If a student makes an error on a word during oral reading, the teacher should not stop and correct it immediately. To do so would prevent natural use of context. If the student reads to the end of a sentence and does not realize through distorted meaning that a mistake has been made, the teacher may then provide the correction.

One technique for teaching initial awareness of context clues is through forced-choice completion of blanks in sentences. Here is an example of the technique:

It was time for lunch. Wyatt had not eaten for many hours. He was very _____.
1) happy   2) hungry   3) angry

The Cloze Procedure, used to assess student reading level, can also be used for remediating context usage. The teacher types out a passage from a book that falls within the child's reading level. Blanks are placed at regular intervals, usually every fifth word, and the student is asked to fill them with words that fit. The words do not have to be exactly the same as the ones left out as long as they mean approximately the same thing; the student is using context.

Students with vision have the advantage of using pictures to understand context clues from many stories. The teacher can substitute a description for the student reading braille so that they, too, may learn to "read between the lines" using pictorial descriptions.

Finally, provide students with ample opportunity to read materials of particular interest to them. Each day the students should be allowed some classroom time for "free reading."

Comprehension

Comprehension is perhaps the most complex of the skills involved in reading. Prior to discussing the specific types of comprehension, several general suggestions will be offered.

General Comprehension

The more a student reads, the better they are likely to comprehend. One of the greatest problems in remediation, however, stems from the aversion to reading most striving readers have developed. How can a student be motivated to practice something at which they have experienced repeated failure? A crucial first step is for the teacher to discover what subjects the student enjoys. This may not be easy, since remedial students are not likely to articulate their interests to their teacher, even when they are specifically asked to do so. One way to obtain this information indirectly is through sentence completion exercises. Read statements such as those below, and ask the students to fill in the blanks:

- After school I like to _____.

- When I have time to daydream, I imagine that I am _____.
- If I could miss a week of school, I would _____.
- My favorite television program is _____.

Once the teacher has determined what the child's interests are, they should find easy reading material on those subjects.

A wide variety of reading materials must be available for the student to browse through and select for free reading time. The teacher might offer to read some books aloud if they are beyond the student's reading level. The remedial student might be asked to confer with the teacher about the number of books they will read each week. When a book is selected initially, the teacher should help the student go through the book to locate troublesome vocabulary words so these can be explained ahead of time.

Even though the student may be having difficulty comprehending what they read, at least one-fourth of the remedial reading time should be spent allowing the student to read silently. The amount of time spent silently reading may be short initially but will increase gradually as the student improves. From time to time, the teacher will need to check the student's comprehension in a nonthreatening manner. Oftentimes, this is accomplished by asking questions related to the student's feelings or emotions.

Rereading material is a helpful remedial technique in comprehension; however, it can be a threatening experience if not carefully planned. Whenever possible, the student should be asked to read a passage silently the first time and orally with a classmate the second time. Comprehension should not always be checked through questioning the student. Instead, the student might record their feelings, dramatize the story, or write a new ending for the story.

Literal Comprehension

Literal, or factual comprehension, often receives too much emphasis in the regular classroom. Remembering the facts of a story should be emphasized as little as possible in the remedial setting. It is important readers of braille learn to outline material for its general content.

The vision teacher should give the students several good models of outlines transcribed into braille. The outlines will ideally cover material the student has already read. Another method of teaching outlining skills is to have a student brainstorm everything they can think of about a hobby or favorite sport. The student is then asked to sequence those facts so they make sense to someone who is trying to learn about the hobby or sport. From the sequence, a simple outline can be framed.

Motivating materials to use for teaching literal comprehension include cookbooks and magazines. The teacher might also clip paragraphs out of stories in old braille books and ask the student to sequence them.

Interpretive Comprehension

When students are unable to interpret the meaning of a story, they may have inappropriate backgrounds for going beyond the exact words on a page. It is the teacher's responsibility to ask questions concerning their general understanding of the subject before attempting to teach the skill of interpretation.

Initially, students should be given several examples of interpretations that have already been made on stories they have read; this will make it easier for them to understand what reading between the lines really means.

The teacher might paraphrase several paragraphs of a story and ask the student to match the paraphrased statement with the original paragraph. A matching exercise might also be done with topic sentences of paragraphs.

During the beginning stages of interpretive reading, it is important the teacher probe for elaboration. This means when students begin to use their own words to describe what they have read, the teacher asks them questions or help to express a partially formed idea.

Critical Thinking and Problem-Solving Comprehension

To go beyond the meaning of the words on a page and to think creatively about content is the highest level of comprehension. Teachers must be very accepting of students' attempts at this process while constantly probing for more originality.

It is often motivating and less threatening to work on critical comprehension in small groups. The group brainstorms on questions such as, "What would happen if the main character in this story had been a girl instead of a boy?" Groups might also work on figures of speech such as "playing it cool." The task would be to guess the meanings.

Reading assignments for teaching critical problem solving must be kept highly interesting. After the student achieves some initial success, content materials they may be reading in the regular classroom can be used for practicing this skill.

Role playing is also a useful activity for children who have difficulty reacting to creative reading. Additionally, asking students to make analogies is another group activity that can help teach critical problem solving after reading.

Rate of Reading

If a student reads braille too slowly, they will not only have trouble keeping pace with print-reading peers but will also become less motivated to read at all. Students read slowly for any number of reasons. Some students scrub vertically up and down the braille dots, others press down too heavily on the dots, while still others are character-by-character readers. In most cases, these slow readers began to memorize the braille code before they developed good mechanical tracking skills. Chapter 4 outlines ways of working on those mechanical skills. Additional ideas for increasing braille reading rates will be discussed later in this chapter where the difficulties of former readers of print are examined.

Flexibility of Reading Rate
Slow readers of braille are also often *inflexible readers*, that is, they read all material at the same rate regardless of difficulty or purpose. Again, Chapter 4 contains many ideas for working on the flexibility of students' braille reading rates. Every idea is applicable to the remedial reader of braille, though the difficulty level of materials used for practicing varying reading rates may have to be lowered for the remedial reader. The contrast between types of reading materials may also need to be accentuated. Open book evaluations are good for helping cautious readers scan reading material for specific information. Later, however, timing and charting reading rates on both skimming and scanning activities will be essential.

Oral Expression
Students of braille who use poor expression during reading aloud can often be helped through *choral reading*, reading aloud in groups. Another worthwhile remedial technique is to play recordings of motivating stories for students during free time. When students write their own language experience stories, they are often able to practice good oral expression more naturally. When students begin to make progress on oral expression, the teacher might introduce the "distortion game." In this game, the teacher reads a story aloud to the student but deliberately distorts its meaning through inappropriate oral expression. The student is then asked to identify the teacher's mistakes and correct them.

Attitude and Motivation
Attitude and motivation are covered quite extensively in Chapters 3 and 4. The reader is also referred to the final section of the present chapter for further suggestions for working with former readers of print. Pacing is perhaps most important when trying to remediate in this area. Students who have developed negative feelings about reading must not be rushed into reading of any kind. There must be time for desensitization to the act of reading. This may mean that the teacher and student spend time talking, walking, and discussing interesting subjects. When the teacher senses that the student is sufficiently relaxed, the teacher might have the student dictate a story based on a recent personal experience. Beyond experience stories, materials about sports, movies, TV characters, and other favorite activities might be transcribed for use. The student might also listen to a recording while reading these braille materials.

Working with Former Readers of Print
If students have had difficulty with reading print, they probably will also have difficulty with braille. Many of the remediation techniques previously discussed in this chapter will be appropriate for these former readers of print. On the other hand, there are some unique factors a teacher must consider when doing remedial work with these students. It is the purpose of this section to discuss those factors and suggest ways to deal with them.

Motivation
The former reader of print most often has a large psychological hurdle to overcome with respect to the loss of sight. Forcing braille instruction on a student before they are psychologically ready is both unwise and wastes time. A sensitive parent or teacher must ascertain how well the child is progressing with respect to accepting their visual loss. When print can no longer be read with maximum magnification or it becomes too fatiguing, braille may be considered. At this point, asking the child what they know about braille and how they feel about it is important. If a braille-reading child of the same age can be located, arranging an informal meeting between them is a good idea. It is ideal if this braille-reading student also once read print, though this kind of match may be difficult to find. If regular tutoring by such a fellow student can be arranged, this may also serve to motivate the former reader of print to approach braille more positively.

The teacher can heighten the student's interest in braille if they help the student make braille labels for personal belongings. The teacher might also braille material the student has memorized or written for examining independently.

Tracking
The mechanics of tracking with the hands will be totally foreign to the former readers of print. The use of simulated materials and repetitious braille discussed in Chapter 4 would be very appropriate for this student, just as it is appropriate for the young child who has not read in a medium other than braille. Precision teaching with the use of rate and accuracy goals can be very helpful for reassuring the student that they are making progress. A readiness program such as the *Mangold Braille Program, Basic Braille Unit 1 & 2* provides teachers with ready-made performance criteria on these mechanical skills. As was emphasized in Chapter 4, mechanical skills need to be well developed before the student is asked to work on discrimination of the braille characters.

Tactile Perception
It will not be necessary to go back as far in this area with the former reader of print as it would be for the young beginning reader of braille. While a short time may be spent detecting gradations of textures or types of fabric, the teacher will want to move rapidly into discrimination of the braille cell. Flash cards and card games are motivating means of drilling letter or word recognition. Whenever possible, flash cards should contain the letter or word in context as well as in isolation. Again, the *Mangold Program* is a helpful set of materials for teaching letter recognition.

If there has been no history of difficulty reading print, and most of the letters have been learned, the student should be started on some high interest, low vocabulary materials. Below is a list of companies and their websites that publish materials of this nature.

- Classic Starts: rainbowresource.com/category/5927/Classic-Starts.html
- Crabtree: crabtreebooks.com/en-ca/products/by-subject/hi-lo-resources-titles/crabtree-chrome
- Great Illustrated Classics: greatillustratedclassics.com/
- High Noon Books: highnoonbooks.com/HNB/HNB-List_Intro.tpl?cart=16225698739759493
- HIP Books: hip-books.com/books/
- Simple Word Books: simplewordsbooks.com/

Speed Building

It is very important that the former reader of print does not become a "scrubber" or an analytical reader. Scrubbing is defined here as moving the fingertips up and down over the braille cells as opposed to sweeping smoothly across them horizontally. An analytical reader may become a *scrubber*, as they attempt to derive meaning from each cell rather than from words or word combinations. If the rate is too slow, the print images of letters are often recalled visually as they come in contact with the corresponding braille symbols. This intermediate association is not good because it will prevent efficient reading in the long term. There are several techniques for building speed with former readers of print. Many of these, of course, are useful to all readers.

Warm-up Tracking

A minimum of 10 minutes should be devoted to warm-up tracking at the beginning of each reading period. This calls for hand movements across and down a page at a rate that allows for no symbol recognition. This can also be a time for the student to practice independent hand movements and new patterns of tracking down a page. Each day, the student should strive to cover more pages in a specified time while still attempting no symbol recognition.

A good way to work gradually into reading for comprehension is to have the student do some bits-and-pieces reading. This type of reading was described in Chapter 4 under the topic of scanning and skimming. The student locates one or two words on a braille page by random pointing. They then track at a rapid pace down the page to find those words again. From these initial words, the student can be asked to find more words in the same way until they have the thread of the story on that page. After several rereadings, the student's rate should not have decreased significantly, while smooth, rapid movements should be feeling more natural.

An additional warm-up exercise is repeated tracking over a familiar sentence or passage. Each rereading should be done at a faster rate than the previous time. This type of practice encourages the student to read in "chunks" as well as to make rapid judgments about the tactual configuration of a word based on its beginning structure and its use in context.

Low-level Material
Material used for speed building should be at least three to four grade levels below the student's independent reading level. This material should be as high in interest as possible. Although some high-interest and low-vocabulary books that are commercially available will be suitable, it might also be advantageous for the teacher to braille some original passages based upon the student's interests and hobbies.

Flash cards of Common Words
Flash cards with the most commonly occurring words should be brailed for the student. Among these words should also be the signpost and turn-about words described in Chapter 4. A nonslip reading pad should be provided for use with flash cards. As previously mentioned, flash cards should have a phrase or sentence that uses the word in context as well as presenting it in isolation. Again, some identification of top and bottom is necessary. This can be achieved by clipping off one corner of the card or simply notching the top of the card.

Recorded Braille
When the student has begun reading in a regular reading series, some of the stories should be recorded. They can then listen to the recordings as they track across the corresponding braille. When they can keep up with the normal speaking rate, the speaking rate should be increased even further. Again, this tactic forces the reader of braille to make rapid associations between the tactual configurations and their meanings in context.

Goal Setting, Timing, and Charting
At each reading period, the student's reading rate should be measured. A goal for the period's end and the next day's session should be set. Timings can be accomplished independently by the student if the teacher records several time intervals with the words "start" and "stop," or uses a preset timer. The timing should begin at 30 seconds, then 1 minute, gradually building up to 5 minutes. The student needs encouragement to record their daily progress and perhaps to construct a tactual graph of progress over time.

Blocking Subvocalizations
When a student is first learning braille, there will be a great temptation to subvocalize words they are reading. Subvocalization not only slows reading rate but also allows the student time to visualize print symbols as an intermediate step between tactual contact and interpretation. In addition to the warm-up exercises previously suggested, the teacher can have the student place a pencil between their front teeth as a reminder not to move their mouth in subvocalization.

References

Bammen, H., Dawson, M., & McGovern, J. (1973). *Fundamentals of basic reading instruction.* McKay.

Brown-Barlow, F., Barker, C., & Harris, M. (2019). Size and modality effects in braille learning: Implications for the blind child from prereading sighted children. *British Journal of Psychology, 89,* 165–176.

Clymer, T. (1963). The utility of phonic generalizations in the primary grades. *The Reading Teacher, 16*(4), 252–258.

Harris, A., & Sipay, E. (1971). *Effective teaching of reading.* New York: McKay.

Herr, S. (1970). *Learning activities for reading.* Wm. C. Brown.

Spache, G. (1972). *The teaching of reading.* Phi Delta Kappa.

Steinman, B. A., LeJeune, B. J., and Kimbrough, B. T. (2006, January). Developmental stages of reading process in children who are blind and sighted. *Journal of Visual Impairment and Blindness, 100*(1).

Wilson, R. (1972). *Diagnosis and remedial reading for classroom and clinic.* Charles E. Merrill.

CHAPTER 6

Adding Spice to a Braille Reading Program with Activities and Games

Introduction
The following chapter was originally written by Sally Mangold for the first edition of *Guidelines and Games*, and her work lives on in this edition; however, terminology updates have been made, games have been supplemented as necessary, and a section on technology has been added.

Adding Spice to a Braille Reading Program
It is impossible to overemphasize the importance of helping children become efficient readers. The ability to read skillfully is becoming increasingly important in every aspect of modern living. It is the responsibility of the schools to provide a well-balanced program, which is designed to help children develop the necessary skills that are essential to everyday life.

A well-balanced reading program includes a variety of reading experiences (e.g., developmental, functional, and recreational). Each makes a significant contribution to the child's learning: A developmental program provides systematic instruction in reading skills; a functional program is concerned with the use of reading skills to accomplish a specific purpose, such as reading to locate information; and recreational reading develops desirable reading interests and stimulates each child to read widely for pleasure, both through books and games.

In this chapter, the use of activities and games as they relate to the recreational aspects of a good reading program is highlighted. Games are a way to provide repeated exposure to appropriate vocabulary, while maintaining a high level of motivation for learning to read. The activities and games suggested in this chapter are described for their appropriateness to numerous skill areas.

Reading Readiness
Reading readiness is a state of general maturity that allows a child to learn to read with understanding and without difficulty. A multimedia, multisensory approach is the most effective at this level. Braille users should be encouraged to use all of their residual vision to explore their environment and complete activities. Following is an outline of the readiness skills that need to be mastered by pre-braille students. These skills may easily be turned into games by giving points to the student for each correct response and giving the teacher a point for each incorrect response.

Activities should be adjusted so that the student wins most of the time.

Determining Likes and Differences
Sorting Objects
- by texture: soft, rough, hard, smooth
- by physical properties: round, square, thick, thin
- by function: items that belong in the bathroom, items that are found in the kitchen, items found in the yard, items used when eating
- by size: items that will fit in a pocket, items that will fit in little bottles and big bottles.

Determining Whether Objects Are the Same or Different
When students are asked to compare two objects, be certain that the questions are specific. An example follows:

Teacher gives student a knife and fork.
Teacher: "Are these two objects the same?"
Student: "Yes."
Teacher: "No, they are different because they are different lengths."

The student may have said, "yes" because they recognized that both the knife and fork were of metal. Always be certain to have the student verbalize the characteristics that make two things the same or different.

- same or different by texture
- same or different by function
- same or different by size

Have the student identify the one object that is different in a large group of objects by using the following examples:

- a peanut mixed in with 10 or 12 walnuts
- a spoon mixed in with a number of forks
- a straw mixed in with a number of pencils

Ask the student to identify the one object that is different from two like objects:

- by texture
- by function
- by size
- by color (when possible)

Developing Meaningful Language
- Ask the children to bring to school toys, souvenirs, collections, or favorite possessions that might be shared with the group. Ask each child to show an object and then tell everyone about it. After the

students understand this activity, ask them all to bring the same type of object on the same day (e.g., a piece of clothing a parent wears to work, a beautiful leaf, a favorite stuffed animal.)

- At this age, sighted students are beginning to detect subtle differences between similar objects. When the teacher provides a student who is visually impaired with an opportunity to compare a number of objects from the same category, they have reduced the student's environment to a manageable size.
- Keep lists of appropriate descriptive words and use as many as possible when the student who is visually impaired is examining different objects. This is the means of building a meaningful vocabulary.
- Read a story to the children; then, ask the children to create a new ending for the story.
- Present the class with an unusual object they would not recognize. Ask them to create a story to explain how the object might be used.
- Have the children make hand puppets with foam balls, using sticks for handles, buttons for eyes, and fabric for ears, which are pinned on with straight pins. Ask the children to create a story about their puppet and where it likes to go.
- Use Potato Head dolls for identifying parts of the body.
- Using hand puppets, have the children create a dramatic play and act out members of their families.
- Play the word-by-word circle game. Have the children sit in a circle, and the teacher or a child start off with a word or name, such as "George." The next child adds another word repeating the first, "George was," and each child adds a new word until a complete sentence has been spoken. The game may be continued until a complete story has been told about George.
- Read the children a three- or four-line story that is unknown and ask them to create an ending for the story (e.g., "Danny and Rick went for a walk in the woods. When they were deep in the woods, they heard a strange sound. They looked back and saw . . .").
- Play a rhyming game. Show the children hand or finger puppets and explain that each small rhyme will end with a word that rhymes with the name of the puppet (e.g., "This little boy is Bill. Bill lives on a ____. This little girl is Sue. Sue's favorite color is ____.").
- Create unique and outlandish rhymes (e.g., "See the cat wearing a hat, the big bad goat ate my ____.").

Developing Motor Control
- Dramatic Plays: Read a story such as *Three Billy Goats Gruff* and have the children act out the story.
- Creating a structure:
  - Construction blocks
  - Simple shape puzzles
  - Use of tools (i.e., saw, hammer, nails)
  - Pegboard
  - Nesting toys
  - Pop-it beads
- Use of outdoor play equipment
- Coloring: Make raised-line shapes by using a tracing wheel on the reverse side of braille paper. The paper is placed on top of a thin piece of cardboard, rubber, or stiff foam. The desired shape is then embossed with the tracing wheel. Students may be asked to color inside of the raised shapes.
- Cutting with scissors: Always use very sharp sewing scissors when the child is cutting under supervision. Be sure to use blunt-nosed scissors when the child is working independently.
  - Give the child a piece of heavy construction paper 1.5 inches wide. Teach the student to cut all the way across and continue cutting until the strip of paper has been cut into many, many tiny pieces. These pieces of paper may be glued down to make a collage.
  - Give the child a strip of construction paper 2 inches wide. Teach the child to cut almost all the way across. Continue making cuts across the strip of paper until they reach the end. Teach the child to roll the cut sections around a pencil to make the sections curl. The two ends may be stapled together to make a headband.

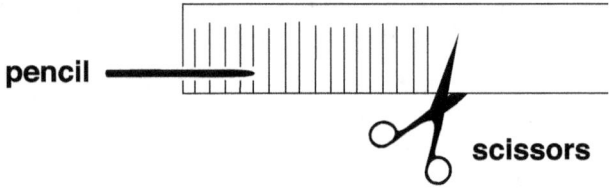

  - Give the student a large piece of construction paper. Have them make cuts all the way around the perimeter of the paper. This could be used as a place mat for a party, or as a decoration on a display table.

- Cut a desired shape out of cardboard (keep it simple). Staple the cardboard shape on top of medium weight construction paper. Teach the student to follow the cut cardboard when using their scissors. After they have cut out a shape by following the shape of the stapled cardboard, remove the cardboard to reveal the construction paper duplicate.
- Folding and tearing paper: Shapes may be made on construction paper using a tracing wheel that has rather large teeth. The student may be taught to tear along this line in order to make the shape that has been drawn.
- Rhythms
  - Hopping, skipping, and running to music
  - Dancing
    - Creative
    - Repeating a pattern that has been taught
    - Dancing with a partner
- Bouncing a large rubber ball
  - Up and down with one's self
  - Back and forth to another person
- Throwing sandbags: An audible target helps focus the direction of the throw. A large board may be made, which contains a number of different sized holes. A radio may be placed behind the board to indicate to the child the direction of the target. For children who have difficulty, use a large box that is placed so that the open side faces the child. Place a radio behind the box to provide an audible indication of the direction of the box.
- Walking a balancing beam
  - Broadside
  - Narrow side

Developing Left or Right Directionality
Pegboards
Use two pegboards, and set up one as a model to show the activity in its final completed form. Teach the student to examine the model by always beginning at the left side and going across each line. This allows the student to work independently when a teacher is not available. The student may keep checking the model to remind them of the desired finished product and can also use the model to check their work when the task is completed.

Model pegboard setup options:

1. Place one peg in each hole, beginning at the left side of each line. Continue all the way across the board.

3. Place one peg in every other hole on each line beginning at the left and going across the board.

4. Place a peg in the first hole and the last hole of each line.

5. Place one peg in the first line, two pegs in the second, three pegs in the third line, etc.

The Magnet and Square Game
Have the student put a self-adhesive fuzzy circle or foam dot inside each square of a sheet of raised-line graph paper, available from American Printing House for the Blind (APH). Always begin at the left margin and go across the page. When the teacher says, "Go," the student begins to put one dot in each square. After 60 seconds the teacher says, "Stop." The student gets one point for each square that contains a dot, and the teacher gets one point for each square that does not contain a dot. The one with the most points wins the game.

Raised Line Game
Roll a sheet of embossed writing paper, available from APH, into a braillewriter. Place a full braille cell at the left end and right end of each line. Then place the paper on the table in front of the student. The student should take a crayon, begin at the left end of the line, and follow the raised line all the way across the page to the full cell at the right side. One point is given for each line that is correctly followed. Many activities for left-to-right sequencing are presented in the *Mangold Basic Braille Program from Exceptional Teaching Aids.*

Tactual Perception

Dominoes
Create large dominoes by placing different patterns of self-adhesive fuzzy dots on heavy tag board or utilize fabric dominoes on a nonslip surface, such as rubber or flannel covered.

Identifying Similar Shapes
Cut heavy cardboard into basic shapes (i.e., circle, square, triangle, rectangle). The student sorts the shapes and puts them in the appropriate slot that has been cut in the top of a shoebox.

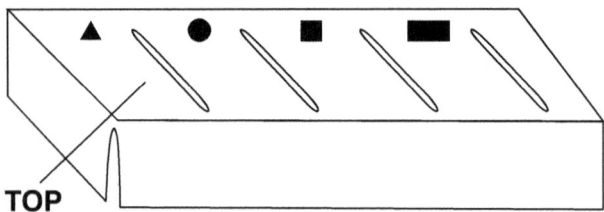

Tape the appropriate shape next to the slot. If the box is covered with contact paper, taped-down shapes may easily be changed for new activities. Variations include using the same shape in four different sizes and textures.

Children who demonstrate the ability to tactually discriminate between textures of like objects in their daily lives and notice the subtle differences in the size and shape of real objects in their envoironment are ready to begin developing tactual perception skills necessary for mastery of braille. Fourteen carefully sequenced lessons, including many games, can be found in the *Mangold Basic Braille Program*. For a more complete description of this program, see Chapter 4.

Developing Auditory Discrimination and Memory
Sounds Around Us

1. Take a walk. Stop and ask the student to listen for 1 minute. Ask the student to dictate a list of things they heard during the minute they were listening. Take another walk on another day and read to the student the list of things they heard on the first day. See how many new sounds they can identify on the second walk.
2. Listen to a recording that contains familiar sounds—telephone, alarm clock, water running, food frying, etc. Many sound effects compilations are available online. Practice identifying the familiar sounds.
3. Tap different surfaces in the classroom and help the student identify the material from which the objects were made. A variation is to tap two or three things in sequence, and the student then tries to identify the objects that were tapped and the order in which they were tapped.
4. Play the tapping game. Select two objects in the room; tap one object very loudly and one very softly. The student is asked to identify the loud sound, then the soft sound. This game may continue with the teacher tapping two things softly and two things loudly, etc.

Sound Blocks

1. Practice in the discrimination of sound may be provided by asking students to discriminate between high and low sound blocks struck with the same mallet. High/low are the easiest to discriminate.
Make a series of high/low sounds and ask the student to repeat the same rhythm saying "High/low" (e.g., High high high, low low low, high high, low low, high low high, high low high).
2. Give the student a number of individual sound blocks to place in sequence with the lowest sound on the left and the highest sound on the right.

Clock and Watch Games

Place a loud ticking alarm clock somewhere in the classroom. Set a timer for 5 minutes and instruct the student to locate the ticking clock. If they find the clock within 5 minutes, they win the game. After the student can locate the loud ticking clock easily, substitute a loud ticking watch or kitchen timer.

Follow the Leader
The student imitates everything the teacher is doing—opening doors, opening drawers, placing a book on the table, pushing a chair under a table, getting a drink of water.

Guess Who I Am
Students line up behind one chair. The child sitting in the chair covers their eyes. The first child standing behind the chair says, "Guess who I am." If the student in the chair guesses correctly, they may have another turn. If they miss, they go to the end of the line. This game helps sighted students in a regular classroom to understand how difficult it sometimes is to recognize people by their voices and helps the student who is visually impaired learn the names of classmates.

Listening for Detail
Tell a short story. Ask the student such questions as:

- What did Jimmy do first when he arrived at the party?
- What was Jimmy's favorite toy?
- How long did Jimmy's mother want him to stay at the park?

Ask students questions such as, "What does the ball do when it is dropped?" Listen for answers like, "Bounce." Ask, "What does the angry dog say?" and listen for, "Bow-wow," or, "Rrrff." After the children understand the game, a student who says a correct answer may make up a question for another student. A number of students may be divided into two teams. One point is given to each team when a member of that team gives a correct answer.

Teaching Pre-primer Concepts
It is vital for a student to understand the concepts that will be presented in the pre-primers. The sighted student obtains many clues about various experiences by looking at the pictorial representations in the reader. A student who is blind, on the other hand, must have actually experienced the activities if they are to benefit from the discussion carried out in the reading circle.

A list of concepts presented in a pre-primer may be compiled and given to the student's parents, so that everyone in the student's learning environment may contribute activities and games that will strengthen the student's understanding of the world in which they live. Examples of typical pre-primer activities are riding a pony, going to the park, riding on a bus, using an umbrella when it rains, helping cook in the kitchen, and going to the store to buy new shoes.

Classroom teachers frequently make large wall charts that contain pictures of all the characters who will be met in the pre-primer story. Small dolls may be provided for the braille user. If the printed names are placed on the wall chart next to the pictures, be certain that a braille label is made for each of the dolls so that the student may become familiar with the configuration of each character's name.

Launching a Formal Reading Program in the Primary Grades

Regarding commonly recorded milestones, holding and manipulating a book is postponed so that the child who reads braille is confronted with only one mechanical task of reading at a time.

Experience Books

The content of these books should reflect the child's experiences. The acquisition of good reading skills is greatly enhanced if the child quickly sees the relationship between the abstract symbols and the real world around them.

Pictures and drawings that illustrate the content of these books reinforce this concept for sighted students. Whenever possible, provide a real object for the braille reader to remind them of the content of the chart.

Examples:

**I like gum.
Gum is good.**

MY NEW SHOES

Shoelace

**I have new shoes.
I like new shoes.
My new shoes are brown.**

After the page is brailled, words in print should be placed above the braille so that the classroom teacher can read the words in print without disturbing the position of the child's hands.

Example: The teacher brings a bird in a cage to show to the students.

**Henry is a bird.
Henry is soft.
I like Henry.
Henry lives in a cage.**

Word and Phrase Charts

Many classroom teachers write new vocabulary and phrases on strips of heavy tag board. The strips are pinned on bulletin boards or placed in pocket charts as they are introduced. A duplicate set of braille strips should be provided for the braille user. The print above the braille should be done in felt-tip pen so sighted children who only read print can participate in many games with braille users. A textured rubber pad or felt-covered board should be placed on the reading surface so the braille cards do not slip easily.

Enrichment Charts

- Calendar
- Rules of the school
- Menus
- Names and classroom helpers
- List of birthdays

Everything found in a classroom and written in print should be brailled and made available to the student who uses braille. Many teachers like to bind the stories or charts together into a small booklet or place them in pockets along the perimeter of a room, at a level where they can be reached by a braille user.

Braille Letter Recognition

Braille letters are introduced in the *Mangold Basic Braille Program* after the student has mastered 14 skills of tactual perception. At that point, exercises that introduce one letter at a time are provided. No reversible pairs are ever introduced simultaneously. The following games from the *Mangold Program* may be used to reinforce letter recognition.

c ⊃	c ⊃	c ⊃
g ϱ	g ϱ	g ϱ
1 ɭ	1 ɭ	1 ɭ

Letter Game

Cut out playing cards, each with a single braille letter in the upper left corner. Use heavy paper or tape them onto cardboard so they do not bend easily. Place the deck of cards with the braille side upwards in a small box on the middle of the table. Each student in turn takes one card from the top of the deck. They must read the braille letter in the upper left-hand corner. If they read the card correctly, they may put that card in front of them on the table. If they do not read it correctly, they must give it to the other player. When all the cards are gone from the deck, the player with the most cards wins the game.

Racing game

Two players sit across the table from one another. Both players locate the thick line in the middle of the page. Both players put a magnet or token in the square that contains the brailled letter "c" in the row nearest to the thick line

p	y	g	c	l
y	p	l	g	c

c	g	l	d	y
l	c	g	y	d

(upper left square). The players take turns rolling the die. They move their token from left to right according to the number on the die. If they can read the letter in the square on which they land, they may stay there. If they cannot read the letter they must go back to the beginning. The first player to move across all of the squares from left to right wins the game.

The Wiggle Worm Game

The page should be placed upon the table so the head of the worm is nearest to the player. Each player will begin the game with a marker in the space to the right of the worm's head and continue moving their token until they reach the tail of the worm. The first player to reach the tail wins the game. The number of spaces each player may move will be indicated by the roll of the die. If the player can read the name of the braille letter on that space, they may stay there; if they cannot read the braille letter they must go back to the beginning space again.

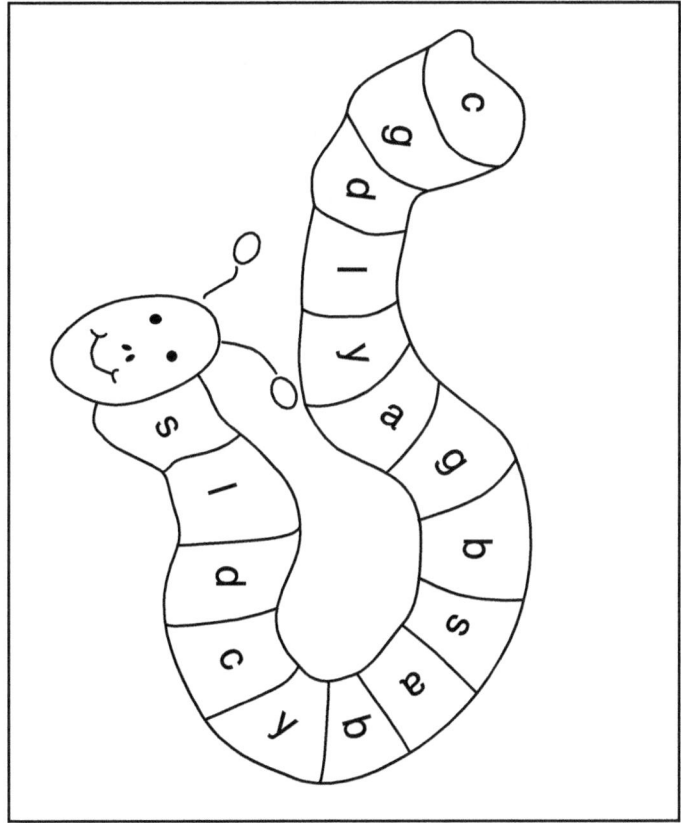

Concentration

Cut out and prepare these playing cards with braille letters. Lay them face down on the table. Each player in turn chooses two cards. If they do not make a match, they must be returned to the same spaces on the table. If they do match, the player keeps them. Each player does this in turn until all the cards have been collected, and whoever has the most pairs wins the game.

g	g	c
c	l	l
d	d	y

Egg Carton Game
The letters in the top two lines should be cut out and attached to the bottom of each cup in an egg carton. Use double-sided tape for attaching the letters. The bottom two lines of letters may be used to prepare a second egg carton. Tape or staple the two egg cartons end to end, with all of the letters pointing in the same direction. Both players sit on the same side of the table. One player will move a marker across the top row, and the other player will use the bottom row. Table tennis balls may be used for markers. The roll of the die indicates how far each player may move. The player must read correctly the letter in the cup where the marker lands. If they do not read it correctly, they must move their marker back three spaces or to the first cup if there are not three spaces. The first player to reach the opposite end of the two cartons wins the game.

g	c	l	d	y	a
b	s	w	p	o	k
g	c	l	d	y	a
b	s	w	p	o	k

Make a Face
Have the student decorate the face below by adding materials for eyes, nose, hair, etc. Put a slit for a mouth on the line indicated.

Cut out the "tongues" with letters on them and use them with the face. Put them through the slit from the back side so the student may read the letters as they come out of the mouth. Attach the tongues to heavier paper if they seem too difficult to handle.

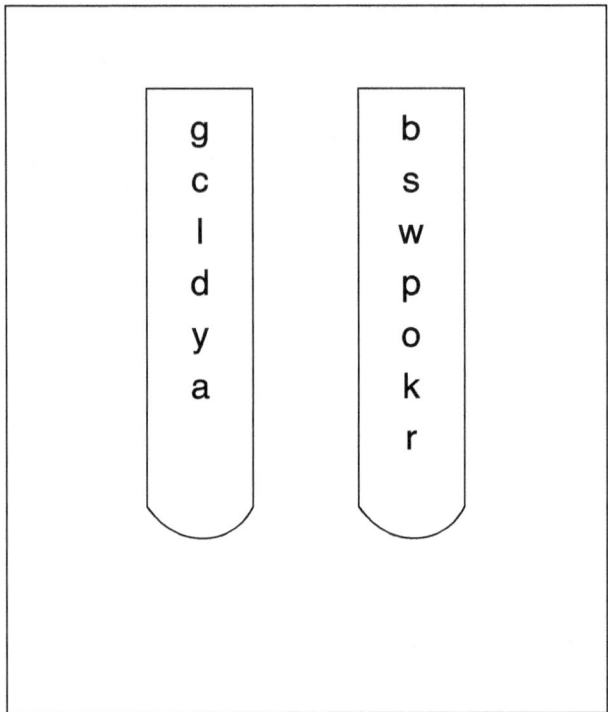

Quick Answer Game

Each of the two players places a game sheet on the magnet board. The first player locates the upper left square, which contains the braille letter "x." The player rolls the die and counts the number of squares indicated. The player must locate the correct square and say aloud the correct letter in that square before the other player counts to 5 seconds. If they say it correctly, they may move the magnet to that square. If they do not say it correctly, they must move back to square one. At the end of a line, players should return to the left side and resume counting on the next line. The first person to move across all three lines of squares and land on the bottom right square (which contains a "d") wins the game.

x	g	n	c	l	h
d	e	y	m	a	r
b	k	s	o	w	d

Letter Bingo

Each player has a card marked off into 25 squares (the large raised-line graph paper from APH may be used). In each square, a letter is placed. A small number of individual cards containing one letter each are brailled. The upper right-hand corner may be cut so the student will orient the card correctly. The teacher shows a single letter card to the student. The student reads the letter bingo card, and if they locate an identical letter, they place a magnet on that letter. When each letter in a row has been marked with a magnet, the student says "Bingo!"

Self-Correcting Letter Game

Make a series of small pages and bind them together as a book. Each of the four lines on the page contains a number and a letter.

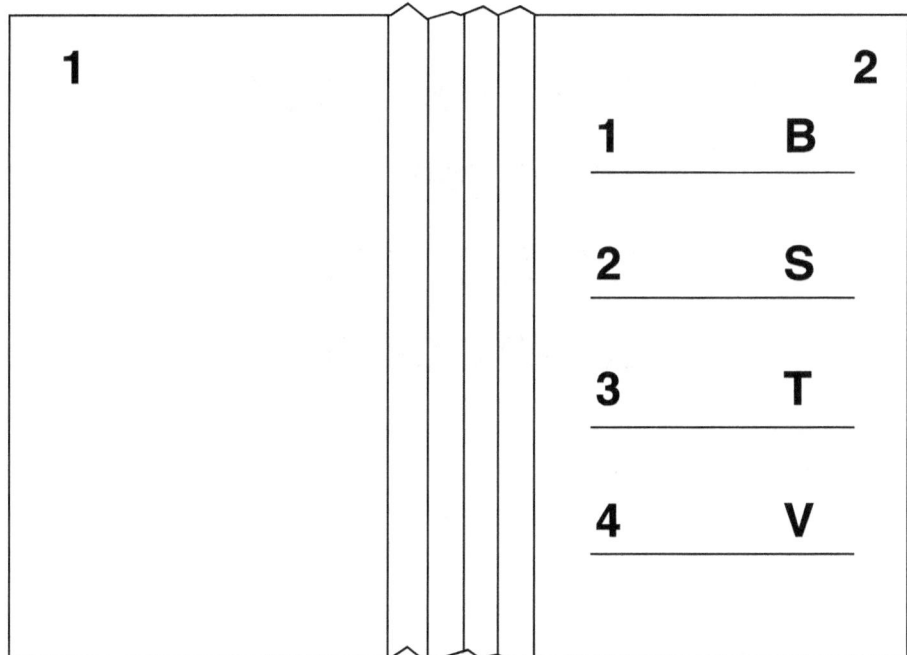

Make a recording following this pattern: "Which number is followed by a letter that sounds like the first sound you hear in *sun?*" . . . *(Pause for student to stop playback, mark an answer, then listen for answer)*. "Answer: 2."

The Shoebox Letter Game

Using the same shoeboxes made earlier for sorting shapes, attach a letter next to the slot in the top of each box. Have a student sort the letters and put them in the appropriate slots. One point is given for each correctly sorted letter. The teacher gets one point for each card that is incorrectly sorted. The one with the most points wins the game.

Treasure Box

The teacher places a box full of objects before the student. Brailled letter cards are taped to the bottom of each cup in a large muffin tin. When the teacher says, "Go," the student removes an object and finds the muffin tin that represents the beginning sound of each object. They then place the object in the correct tin. One point is given for each correctly placed object.

Word Recognition

This provides practice for initial consonant sounds in words. Mark the words that begin with the same sound as the object on top of the page.

GUM

go, see, get, mother, ball, ride, goat, coat

Words That Start the Same

Mark the word that begins like the first word in each line. Examples include:

- Jump, run, play, Judy
- Ball, coat, ride, big
- Mother, tip, go, my, see

Fishing for Words

Word cards are brailled, folded, and pinned shut with a large straight pin. Be sure to use steel pins or hair pins because a magnet will not pick up ordinary pins. The pinned cards are placed in a large fishbowl. The child lowers a piece of string with a small magnet attached to the string into the fishbowl and pulls out a "fish." If the child can read the card correctly, they may keep it. If they cannot read the card correctly, the card goes into another fishbowl to be used at a later time. The fish that are caught may be strung on a piece of fishing line and hung by a pin from the bulletin board. Each day the child reads the "fish" caught the day before, and then tries to catch other fish that are left in the bowl.

Words Category Game

Flash cards are made using the student's reading vocabulary. The upper-right corner may be clipped off so the student will orient the card when it is placed on the rubber pad in front of them. Three milk cartons are taped together and placed at the top of the rubber pad. The student is told that each card belongs in a category and they should place the card in the correct box as shown:

1. Things people can do: see, ride, go, jump, sleep
2. Names of people: Mother, Father, Sue, Tim, Maya, Kenny
3. Names of things: car, skate, house, box, ball

The student is given one point for each correct response.

Treasure House Game

This game may be played after the student has mastered initial and final consonant sounds and short vowel sounds. The student is given a small wooden chest full of familiar objects. A treasure house (18-by-18-inch box, which has dividers placed inside). Short vowel sounding words are brailled and taped to the bottom of each square. The student is directed to select an object from the treasure chest and place it where it belongs in the treasure house. A point is given for each correctly placed object.

Wheel of Fortune

A large circle is cut out of cardboard. The vocabulary words from the student's reader are brailled and taped around the edge of the circle. The circle is attached to a sturdy piece of cardboard with a loose-fitting brad placed in the center. A large cut arrow points from the bottom of the cardboard up toward the center of the circle at the bottom. The wheel is spun and when it stops the student is asked to read the word nearest the tip of the arrow. The student is given one point for each word read correctly.

Word Families

Introduce the notion of word families:

- "ame" family: game, same, came, name
- "ill" family: pill, Phil, Bill, hill

Attach a family name to each pocket in a notebook containing a series of pockets.

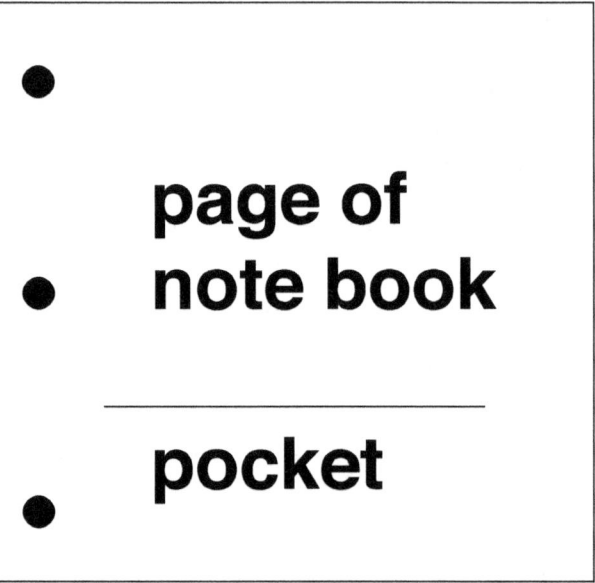

Labeling

It is impossible to provide those who use braille with the quantity of exposure to writing that is provided the sighted child, so every opportunity to use daily experiences must be taken. Teachers should label with braille: (a) toys that children bring from home; (b) areas of the classroom (e.g., shelves and their purpose, fun books to read, math books, science books, etc.); and (c) drawers according to contents (i.e., scissors, paper, pencils, crayons, rulers, etc.).

Labeling at home helps the braille user begin to organize their environment at home and in the classroom. The family may have basic canned goods that they buy frequently; if so, encourage them to put braille labels on the appropriate shelf areas (e.g., beans, tuna, soups.) When they bring food home from the store the student who is visually impaired can help put away the groceries. Some parents use magnetic labels and attach labels to each of the canned goods. Other frequently used areas in the home may be labeled. Favorite books, records, or CDs may be labeled, and tools in the garage may be identified by labels.

Sentence Recognition
Individualized Stories
Each student may dictate a made-up story for the teacher to transcribe. Simplify the vocabulary so that it is appropriate for the child to read. The child may then read this story to another classmate or record it to share with someone else in story time. These stories may be bound in small booklets and illustrated or decorated with appealing tactile items.

Sentences that can be written in one line of print often require two or more lines in braille. Words should be grouped in meaningful phrases. Never break a phrase at the end of a braille line. Never hyphenate words in the primary grades until hyphenation has been introduced in their reader. The vocabulary in a reading chart should be controlled so that it corresponds as closely as possible to that found in the reader.

Answering Questions with Phrases
After children have had a story read to them, they are given phrases brailled on strips of paper. The student is then asked to find the answer to a question such as, "Where did the little boy go?" The student would be expected to pick out a phrase such as, "into the house."

The Rocket Ship
A number is attached to each pocket in a pocket notebook. A cutout of Earth is labeled and placed on the front cover; a cutout of the Moon is labeled and placed on the back cover. Tell the child they will take a trip to the Moon. They will stop at many space stations along the way. Cut simple rocket shapes out of medium-weight cardboard; attach a small pocket to each rocket. Tell the children each rocket will carry a different payload each day. Payloads may be as follows: (1) things people can do—sleep in a bed, walk into a house. (2) things people cannot do—sit in the sky, fly like a bird, swim like a fish. (3) silly sentences—"A cat can fly," "Gum can jump," "Elephants are little."

The Big Family
Provide concentrated exposure to the same word if it is difficult for the student to remember. For example, tell the student each sentence that contains the word "big" is a member of the Big family. Ask the student to read the following sentences and locate the one sentence that does not belong to the Big family.

- The dog is big.
- The house is big.
- The girl has a big kitten.
- The big kitten is yellow.
- The big dog is black.

- The girl is big.
- I see the kitten.

Riddles

Braille a short riddle onto a 5-by-8-inch card and the answer on the other side. This makes the activity self-correcting, for example:

Front of card: I am little. I am gray. I have a long bushy tail. My home is in a tree. I like to eat nuts. What am I?
Back of card: I am a squirrel.

Comprehension

Select three small dolls or action figures to represent three characters from the reader. Place the dolls or action figures on the desk in front of the children. Place a milk carton next to each doll. Attach a card with the name of the doll to each of the corresponding cartons. Give the student a box containing a number of sentence strips. Ask the student to read each sentence and then put it into the box next to the character who is represented by the action in the sentence, as shown:

Have the student determine which character made the cookies, climbed a tree, or has a red dress.

Yes or No

Answer the questions by marking "Yes," or "No." Examples are shown.

- Does a bug have legs? Yes or No
- Can a bird fly? Yes or No
- Can a rabbit fly like a bird? Yes or No
- Can a bird hop like a rabbit? Yes or No

Fluency Practice (reading rate)

Before a teacher begins a fluency activity, they must review, with the student, the definition of fluency and the reason why practice is necessary to become a fluent reader.

What is "fluency"?

- Gliding fingers, soft touch
- Reading not too fast and not too slow
- Reading with expression
- Paying attention to punctuation
- Reading smoothly, not choppy

Why do we practice fluency?

- To help us understand what we are reading
- To become strong braille readers

Charting Fluency with Repeated Reads

Present a short braille passage to the student and practice reading the passage with them one time together, discussing any unknown words. After they have had a chance to practice the passage, tell them they will be timed to see how many words they can read per minute. After they read the passage the first time, see if they can beat their time the second time. Take the best time and chart it. Make sure to add the date and the correct words read per minute so they can see their progress over time. This is a great way for them to have ownership of their learning. Use the same passage for a couple of days or a new passage every day. This can be done with younger readers who are learning letters as well. Have small braille sheets that include letters or words that they have been practicing. Another fun thing is to let the students do fluency reads with a partner. Print can be added to the braille passages if needed.

Fun ways students can chart their own fluency so they can see their growth over time include:

- Stickers: Use puffy stickers on tactile graph paper.
- Bar Graphs: Create a bar graph on the brailler using full braille cells for the bar.
- Snap Cubes: Use one cube to represent each correct word read, and snap them together to create a tower of cubes. It will be fun to compare the towers each day to show growth.
- Small unit cubes: Using an organizer tray that has different compartments, (e.g., a 3-by-3 divided tray), put the cubes in one of the compartments to stand for how many words were read that day.
- Beads on a pipe cleaner: The beads may stand for one word or multiple words. Each bead could be worth two, five, or 10 words. Round up the words per minute achieved.

Repurpose Classic Board Games

This requires a stack of braille cards with letters, words, or phrases on them that support whatever goal the student is working on, such as tracking, sight words, letters, or specific contractions. A tactile die to roll and two players are needed.

Player A will roll the die and announce the number on it. This is the number of braille cards both players need to read. Whoever reads their braille cards first gets to move their game piece. This is a game of speed. If students are not evenly matched with fluency, use a timer instead of racing against each other. The following games may be easily repurposed:

- *Ticktacktoe:* The teacher can find tactile ticktacktoe games at many stores and online, or the teacher can easily make one with puff paint for the game board and coins (or other objects) as the "x"'s and "o"'s. Whichever player reads their cards the fastest will get to add their piece to the board. Whoever has three in a row wins.
- *Trouble:* The teacher can play with up to four players. Add textures or puff paint to the game pieces so players can easily identify which piece is theirs. With a tactile die, the players can move the number of spaces shown on the die if they correctly read their cards quickly. The teacher can use one game piece per player or more.
- *Connect Four:* Add textures or puff paint to the game pieces so players can easily identify which pieces are theirs. Whoever reads their words or phrases first gets to add a piece to work towards getting four in a row.

Pile of Coins

The objective of the game is to read faster than the other players. Give a stack of braille cards and an ice cube tray to each player (2–3 players total). Put a pile of cards in the middle of the playing area. The first player rolls the die and reads the number on the die out loud. Each player will read one braille card at the same time. Whoever reads their card the fastest (and reads it correctly) gets to take coins from the center pile in the amount shown on the die and place them in their tray (one coin per space on the tray). The goal is to get 12 coins (or 24 if playing with two trays each) first. If someone rolls a one, the person who rolled loses all of their coins. If someone rolls a 5, whoever reads their card the fastest on that turn takes their winning coins from their opponent instead of the center pile. A variation could be increasing the number of coins needed (e.g., the first player to 40 wins).

Required materials:

- large handful of coins (or any small counters)
- ice cube trays (one for each player) or another system to track of how many coins each player has
- stack of braille cards that have words or braille letters that meet the objectives of the student
- tactile die

Alternate scoring organization methods:

- egg cartons cut to be used for rows of 10
- fishing tackle organizers, which hold more coins
- strips of papers that have rows of 10 in puffy paint
- beads on strings instead of coins

- blocks that snap together instead of coins
- Score Card Set from APH instead of coins

Integrating Technology: Refreshable Braille Displays
Early experience using a refreshable braille display can inspire confidence with braille displays and help show students that technology can be fun and functional.

Use refreshable braille display to support fluency games
Pre-teaching will need to happen so that the student knows how to scroll through words on their list. Start by simply showing them how to proceed to the next words on the list using their device.

In addition to using braille word cards for fluency games, use those same word lists by typing them onto a computer or notetaker. The student can practice reading the words, letters, or phrases on a refreshable braille display. Fluency games can help students become accustomed and comfortable with reading information on a display. The teacher can put one word per line or more depending on the experience level of the student with refreshable braille technology.

Braille displays can be used to practice the mechanics of reading braille, such as tracking.

Activities for Intermediate Grades
The reading program in the intermediate grades is designed to foster mature reading skills and maintain a high interest in reading. Many students will continue to need help in basic reading skills until the skills are mastered. Other students will be ready to apply their acquired skills for a number of different purposes.

Countless reading activities and games that may easily be adapted into braille may be found in reading guides designed for use with sighted intermediate grade students. At this level, students often enjoy creating their own games.

Summary and Conclusions
A complete program of reading instruction must include developmental, functional, and recreational reading activities. Traditionally, most programs of reading instruction for the braille user have focused on the developmental and functional reading skills. Means must be found to provide recreational reading activities that reinforce and maintain formally introduced skills and also promote a high level of motivation for learning to read.

To provide a more appropriate reading environment for young braille users, researchers need to collect data and teachers need to make observations relevant to the following questions:

1. Are there skills of braille reading that require specific instruction that is not found in the curriculum of the general education classroom?

2. To what extent do braille signs and contractions influence the acquisition of good braille reading skills?

3. During the reading period in the general education classroom, what proportion of time do sighted children spend on recreational reading activities?

4. During which reading activities in the general education classroom are students with visual impairments, most often *not* participating?

5. What kinds of materials must be provided to general education classroom teachers in order to mainstream students who are visually impaired more fully?

References

Burns, P. C., & Schell, L. M. (1969). *Elementary school language arts: Selected readings.* Rand McNally.

Carter, H. L. J., & McGinnis, D. J. (1970). *Diagnosis and treatment of the disabled reader.* MacMillan.

Forte, I., MacKenzie, J., & Frank, M. (1973). *Kids' stuff, reading and language experiences, Intermediate-junior high.* Incentive Publications.

Forte, I., & MacKenzie, J. (1972). *Nooks, crannies, and corners: Learning centers for creative classrooms.* Incentive Publications.

Heilman, A. W., & Holmes, E. A. (1968). *Smuggling language into the teaching of reading.* Charles E. Merrill.

Huck, C., & Kuhn, D. Y. (1968). *Children's literature in the elementary school.* Holt, Rinehart, and Winston.

Mangold, S. (1980). *Touch and color.* Exceptional Teaching Aids.

Myers, R. E., & Torrance, E. P. (1965). *Can you imagine?* Ginn and Company.

Petty, W. T., & Bowen, M. (1967). *Slithery snakes and other aids to children's writing.* Appleton, Century, Crofts.

Platts, M. E. (1973). *Spice: A handbook of classroom ideas to motivate the teaching of the primary language arts.* Educational Service.

Appendix A
Nonfactual Questions for Checking Comprehension

Factual questions, more commonly referred to as questions for literal comprehension, are not difficult for teachers to formulate. Below is a list of questions of a nonfactual nature that can help teachers individualize reading for their students.

1. What happened in the story that happened to you?
2. How is the life of the main character most like your own life? How is their life least like your own life?
3. Have you known people like those in this story?
4. What things that happened in this story would you like to have happen to you?
5. What character in the story would you like to be? Why?
6. How is this book more or less interesting than TV?
7. How did this book make you feel?
8. If you could have changed something about this story, what would it be?
9. Have you read another book similar to this before? How were they alike?
10. What was something in the book you were unable to understand?
11. If this story were being read aloud, who would be the audience?
12. Did the book teach you a lesson of any kind? If so, what was it?
13. Who else in your class would you recommend read this book?
14. Can you say something good or bad about the book in one sentence?
15. Sometimes we say the opposite from what we mean. Example: A person who is giant in stature is nicknamed "Tiny." Did this happen in your book? If so, give an example.
16. Make up another title for your book.
17. Was there any exaggeration in your story?
18. Did any words or sentences the author used make you think of something other than what they were talking about?
19. If you helped someone else get ready to read this book, what would you say?
20. Did anyone in the story speak differently from you or your parents?

21. What could you guess about the characters in this story that is not told about them?
22. What was the author trying to do in this book?
23. What kind of experience would a person have to have before they could write a book like this?
24. When some people like or don't like a book, they say things like: "It hit me hard," or, "It made me sick." Can you use language like this about your book?

Appendix B
Worksheet Ideas for Developing Braille Tactile Skills

The following ideas from Texas School for the Blind and Visually Impaired's *Elementary Reading Skills Continuum* are intended for the teacher to braille in the form of worksheets. Students should be given worksheets before any introduction to braille letter recognition.

1. Format: Horizontal lines of braille dots (2,5) with regular breaks between them.

    a. Directions to Student: Track across the lines and verbalize "break" each time a break occurs.

2. Format: Same as #1 except with irregular breaks.

3. Format: Groups of horizontal dots (1,4) and (3,6).

    a. Directions to Student: Track across the lines and tell whether the dots are high or low.

4. Format: Same as #3 except intermingle several breaks among the braille characters.

    a. Directions to Student: Track across the lines and tell whether there is a high symbol, low symbol, or break.

5. Format: Horizontal lines of dots (1,4), (2,5), and (3,6).

    a. Directions to Student: Track across the lines and tell whether dots are high, low, or middle dots.

6. Format: Same as #5 except intermingle several breaks among the braille characters.

    a. Directions to Student: Track across the lines and tell whether there is a set of high, low, or middle dots, or a break.

7. Format: Rows of braille dots (1,3), (4,6), (1,6), and (3,4).

    a. Directions to Student: Tell whether the dots are straight up and down or slanted.

8. Format: Rows of braille dots (1,3), (4,6), (1,2), (2,3), (4,5), and (5,6).

    a. Directions to Student: Track across the lines and tell whether the dots are close together or far apart.

9. Format: Rows of braille dots (1,3), (4,6), (1,2), (2,3), (4,5), (5,6), (1,6), and (3,4).

    a. Directions to Student: Track across the braille lines and tell whether the dots are straight up and down and close together, straight up and down and far apart, or slanted.

10. Format: Rows of braille dots (1,6), (1,5), (3,4), (2,4), (3,5), and (2,6).

    a. Directions to Student: Track across the lines and tell whether the dots are slanted and close together or slanted, and far apart.

11. Format: Rows of braille dots (1,6), (2,4), (1,5), (5,6), (1,2), (3,5), (2,6), (1,3), (4,6), (1,3), and (3,4).

    a. Directions to Student: Track across the lines and tell whether the dots are slanted and close together, slanted and far apart, straight up and down and close together, or straight up and down and far apart.

12. Format: Row of braille dots (1,3), (1,6), (2,4), (1,5), (5,6), (1,2), (3,5), (2,3), (4,5), and (2,5).

    a. Directions to Student: Track across the lines and tell whether the dots are "slanted," "straight up and down," or "side by side."

13. Format: Rows consisting of two cells followed by a space, with dots 1,2,3 in the first cell and some combination of two of these three dots in the second cell.

    a. Directions to Student: Track across the lines and tell whether the missing dot in the second cell is a high, low, or middle dot.

14. Format: Rows containing two braille cells followed by a space, in which the first cell is a full cell and the second cell contains only 5 dots in various combinations.

    a. Direction to Student: Track across the lines and tell whether the missing dot is on the right or left side, and then, high, low, or middle.

15. Format: Rows of braille cells consisting of various numbers of dots.

    a. Directions to Student: Identify verbally the number of dots in each cell.

16. Format: Rows of braille cells arranged in the following order: Full cell, (4,5,6), (1,2,3), full cell.

    a. Direction to Student: Verbally count the number of cells in each row.

Note. The teacher will initially want to double space between the rows of braille characters on the worksheets. Students who are achieving 100 percent accuracy on a particular worksheet may wish to time themselves and record their rate of progress each day. Texas School for the Blind and Visually Impaired. (1978). *Elementary Reading Skills Continuum.*

https://www.tsbvi.edu/attachments/read_continuum.pdf

Index

activities and games, 73–98. *See also specific activities and games by name*
  attitude and motivation improvement, 35, 68–70
  auditory discrimination and memory, 79–80
  auditory sense stimulation, 26–27
  comprehension skill development, 48–50, 65–68, 94
  contextual reading, 64–65
  decoding skill development, 45–47
  finger dexterity and wrist flexibility, 36
  fluency practice, 94–97
  former print readers, 68–70
  hand movements and finger positions, 36–40, 59–61
  for intermediate grades, 97
  kinesthetic-tactile learning, 24–26
  for launching formal primary grade reading program, 81–83
  left or right directionality development, 77–78
  light finger touch, 40–41, 59
  likes and differences determination, 74–75
  locating skills, 58
  motor abilities development, 76–77
  object comparison, 74–75
  oral expression, 68
  orientation to page, 40
  overview of, 4–5, 73
  phonetic analysis, 61–63
  pre-primer concepts, 80
  for primary grade reading program launch, 81–82
  reading rate improvement, 15–16, 68, 70–71, 94–95, 97
  reading readiness, 73–77
  reading style development, 51–52
  remedial (*see* remedial reading interventions)
  scan reading, 50
  sentence recognition, 93–94
  skim reading, 50–51
  structural analysis, 63–64
  symbol recognition, 41–42, 45–46, 59–61, 70, 83, 92
  tactile perception and discrimination, 41–44, 69–70, 78–79, 81–92, 101–102
  technology integration in, 97
  vocabulary development, 47–48, 82–83
All Aboard! The Sight Word Activity Express, 49
Alphabetic Braille and Contracted Braille Study (ABC Braille Study), 11, 15, 16, 63
alphabet letters, introducing, 41, 44. *See also* symbol recognition
American Foundation for the Blind, 24
American Printing House for the Blind, 13, 17, 25–26, 49, 58, 78, 89, 97
answering questions with phrases activity, 93
Ashcroft's Programmed Instruction Companion Reader: Unified English Braille, 1
Ashcroft's Programmed Instruction: Unified English Braille, 1
assessment of braille skills, 43–44, 57–58
attitude and motivation, 35–36, 68
auditory discrimination and memory, 79–80
auditory sense stimulation, 26–27. *See also* recordings; sound-symbol relationship awareness

Barbier, Charles, 6
basic concept development, 29–30
beginning braille instruction.
   See teaching braille reading
Big family activity, 93–94
bits-and-pieces reading, 51, 70
board games, repurposing classic, 95–96
Boehm 3 Test of Basic Concepts, 30
book handling and position, 52, 58
Bookshare, 45
Braille, Louis, 6
Braille Authority of North America (BANA), 6–7, 54
Braille Blaster, 13
Braille Brain: A Braille Training Program for Educators and Family Members, 1–2, 17–18
braille code
   development of standardized, 6–7
   knowledge of, 1–2
   memorization of rules for using, 47
braille embossers, 13–14
Braille FUNdamentals: UEB, 17
braille reading
   activities and games on (*see* activities and games)
   advice for best results, 10
   alternatives to, 14–15
   assessment of skills in, 43–44, 57–58
   attitude and motivation toward, 35, 36, 68
   awareness of, developing, 30–32
   background on, 4, 6–18
   braille code and, 1–2, 6–7, 47
   braille production for, 13–14 (*see also* transcription into braille)
   carryover skills for, 52–55
   comprehension skills for, 48–50, 65–68, 94, 99–100
   contracted *vs.* uncontracted, 10–11, 16, 41, 46, 59, 62–64
   current state of, 11–12
   decoding skills for, 34–36, 45–47 (*see also* phonetic analysis)
   ergonomics and, 45 (*see also* book handling and position; posture)
   by former print readers, 57, 68–70
   in general education setting, 1, 34–36, 52–55, 98
   importance for literacy, 14–15
   kinesthetic skills for, 44–45
   mechanical skills for, 36–41, 59–60, 67, 69 (*see also* fingers; hands)
   memorized material and, 31–32, 47–48, 59, 69
   modeling good, 31, 34–35
   object labeling and, 35, 69, 80, 92
   overview of background, 4
   paperless, 11–13
   rapid reading techniques, 15, 34–56
   reading rates, 15–16, 67–68, 71, 94–97
   reading style for, 51–52
   remedial reading interventions for, 5, 57–71
   resources on, 17–18
   standardized braille code development, 6–7
   studies on reading habits, 10–11
   tactile perception and discrimination in, 41–44, 69–70, 78–79, 81–92, 101–102
   tactual reading and, 7–9
   teaching (*see* teaching braille reading)
   technology innovations and, 11–14, 15, 97–98
   transcription of print for (*see* transcription into braille)
Braille Too: The Next Generation, 17
braillewriters, 2

Building on Patterns: Primary Braille Literacy Program, 17

Canadian National Institute for the Blind (CNIB), 2
carryover skills, 52–55
charting fluency, 95
choral reading, 68
clock and watch games, 79
Cloze Procedure, 65
compound words, 63–64
comprehension
    activities and games for, 48–50, 65–67, 94
    critical thinking and problem-solving, 67
    evaluation, 48
    general, 65–66
    inferential, 48
    interpretative, 66–67
    literal or factual, 49, 66, 99–100
    nonfactual questions for checking, 99–100
    reading methods for, 3–4
    remedial reading interventions for, 57–71
    teaching to develop, 51–52
compressed speech devices, 14
concentration game, 86
concept development, 29–30. *See also* pre-primer concepts
Connect Four game, 96
Consonant Lotto, 63
contextual reading, 64–65
contracted braille, 10–11, 16, 31, 35, 62–63
critical thinking, 67
curriculum, 17–18

decoding skills, 34–36, 45–47. *See also* phonetic analysis
directionality development, 77–78
Dolch Word List, 49, 51, 63
dominoes, 78
Duxbury Braille Translator (DBT), 13

egg carton game, 87
emergent literacy skills, 21
ergonomics, 45. *See also* book handling and position; posture
evaluation comprehension, 48
experience books and stories, 41, 47, 59, 68, 81–83

figure-ground perception, 28
fingers
    curvature of, 36, 59
    dexterity of, 36
    light touch with, 40–41, 59
    positions for, teaching, 36–40
    scrubbing with, 41, 42, 59, 67, 70
fishing for words game, 91
flexibility skills, 50–51, 68
fluency, 3, 94–97. *See also* reading rates
Follow the Leader game, 80
former print readers, 57, 68–70

general education setting
    adequate braille reading skill development for, 34–35
    carryover skill development for, 52–55
    general education teachers in, 1, 52
    questions on braille reading in, 98
Guess Who I Am game, 80
Guidelines for the Transcription of Early Educational Materials from Print to Braille, 54
gustatory sense development, 28–29

Hadley workshops and courses, 2
hands. *See also* fingers
    movements of, 36–40, 59
    relaxation of, 59
    tracking with (*see* tracking)
    two-handed reading approach, 7, 9, 10, 15–16, 38, 42–44

hand-under-hand guidance, 24, 35
Haüy, Valentin, 6
human attachment, 21–22

individualized stories, 93. *See also* experience books and stories
Individuals with Disabilities Education Act (IDEA), 31
inferential comprehension, 48
intermediate grades, activities for, 97
International Council on English Braille (ICEB), 6–7
International Phonetic Alphabet Braille Code, 7
interpretative comprehension, 66–67

Joint Uniform Braille Committee (JUBC), 6

kinesthetic skills, 44–45
kinesthetic-tactile learning, 24–26. *See also* tactile perception and discrimination

labeling with braille, 31, 35, 69, 80, 92
left or right directionality development, 77–78
Lego Braille Bricks, 60
letter bingo, 89
letter game, 89–90. *See also* self-correcting letter game; shoebox letter game
letter recognition. *See* symbol recognition
Liblouis, 13
light finger touch, 40–41, 59
Listening for Detail game, 80
literal comprehension, 48, 66, 99–100
locating skills, 58
locomotion, 23

magnet and square game, 78
make a face game, 87–88
Mangold Basic Braille Program from Exceptional Teaching Aids, 44, 78
Mangold Braille Program: Basic Braille, 37–40, 42–44, 59, 69, 79, 83
mechanical skills. *See also* fingers; hands
 for braille reading, 36–40, 41, 59, 67, 69
 finger dexterity and wrist flexibility, 36
 former print readers developing, 68–70
 hand movements and finger positions, 36–40, 59–61
 light finger touch, 40–41, 59
 orientation to page, 40
 reading rate and, 67–68
 remedial reading interventions for, 57–59, 68
 tracking as, 37–44, 59, 68, 69, 70, 97
memorized material, 31–32, 47–48, 59, 69
Missouri School for the Blind, 6
morphology, 63
motivation, 68–69
motor development. *See* sensory-motor abilities development
Mountbatten Brailler, 12
Music Braille Code, 7

National Library Service for the Blind and Print Disabled, Library of Congress, 1
Nemeth Braille Code for Mathematics and Science Notation, 7
NextSense Institute, 18

objects
 comparison of, 74–75
 discovery of, 22–23

labeling with braille, 31, 35, 69, 80, 92
sorting, 36, 74
olfactory sense development, 28–29
Optical Character Recognition (OCR) software, 14
optophones, 14
oral expression, 68
orientation to page, 40
outlining skills, 66

pegboards, 77–78
Perkins Brailler, 12, 22
Perkins SMART Brailler, 12
phonemic awareness, 3
phonetic analysis, 61–63
phonics instruction, 3
Phonics We Use Learning Games, 63
pile of coins game, 96–97
posture, 11, 21, 45, 58
precision teaching, 42–44, 69
prefixes and suffixes, 63–64
pre-primer concepts, 80
preschool experiences, 21–31
    basic concept development, 29–30
    early sensory-motor abilities development, 21–23
    emergent literacy skill development, 21
    overview of, 4, 32
    reading awareness, 30–31
    sensory acuity and efficiency development, 23–29
problem-solving comprehension, 67

quick answer game, 88

racing game, 84–85
raised line game, 78
rapid reading techniques, 15, 34–56
reading awareness, 30–31
reading interventions. *See* remedial reading interventions

reading methods
    bits-and-pieces reading, 51, 70
    choral reading, 68
    comprehension, 3–4
    contextual reading, 64–65
    fluency development, 3
    phonemic awareness, 3
    phonics instruction, 3
    rapid reading techniques, 15, 34–56
    reading by listening, 14 (*see also* recordings)
    rereading and repeated reading, 16, 49, 51, 59, 66, 70, 95
    scan reading, 50, 68, 70
    science of reading, 2–4
    skim reading, 50–51, 68, 70
    tactual reading, 7–9 (*see also* braille reading)
    vocabulary instruction, 3
reading rates, 15–16, 68, 70–71, 94–95, 97
reading readiness, 73–77
reading style, 51–52
recordings, 14, 45, 46, 49, 51, 55, 60, 68, 71, 90
refreshable braille devices, 11–13, 15, 97
remedial reading interventions, 57–71
    attitude and motivation improvement, 68
    book handling and posture, 58
    comprehension, 65–68
    contextual reading, 64–65
    finger curvature and hand relaxation, 36, 59
    flexibility skills, 68
    for former print readers, 57, 68–70
    general remediation needs, 57–58
    hand movements, 59
    lightness of touch, 59
    locating skills, 58

remedial reading interventions (*cont.*)
   oral expression, 68
   overview of, 5, 57
   phonetic analysis, 61–63
   reading rate improvement, 68, 70–71
   striving readers, 57–72
   structural analysis, 63–64
   symbol recognition, 59–61
   techniques for, 58
rereading and repeated reading, 16, 49, 51, 59, 66, 70, 95
riddles, 94
rocket ship activity, 93
Royal Institution for Blind Youth, 6

scan reading, 50, 68, 70
screenboards, 41
screen reading software, 14–15, 27
scrubbing, 41, 42, 59, 67, 70
self-correcting letter game, 89
sensory acuity and efficiency development
   auditory sense stimulation, 26–27
   kinesthetic-tactile learning, 24–26
   olfactory and gustatory sense development, 28–29
   overview of, 23–24
   visual sense development, 27–28
sensory-motor abilities development
   activities and games for, 76–77
   human attachment, 21–22
   locomotion, 23
   object discovery, 22–23
   overview of, 21
sentence recognition, 93–94
shapes
   braille book, 35, 48
   braille cell, 7, 8, 12, 42, 60, 69, 70
   concept development and, 30
   figure, 54
   kinesthetic-tactile learning with, 25–26
   letter, 7, 9
   motor development activities with, 76–77
   object, 23
   tactual activities identifying similar, 78–79
shoebox letter game, 90
sight words, 45, 49, 50, 95
sign-post words, 50
skim reading, 50–51, 68, 70
slate and stylus, 2
smell sense development, 28–29
Sound Blocks, 79
Sounds Around Us activity, 79
sound-symbol relationship awareness, 45–46. *See also* phonetic analysis
speech synthesizers, 12, 14
Speech to Print Phonics, 63
striving reader interventions. *See* remedial reading interventions
structural analysis, 63–64
subvocalizations, 51, 71
symbol recognition, 41–42, 45–46, 59–61, 70, 83, 92

tachistoscopes, 15, 41
Tactile Editing Marks Kit, 58
tactile-kinesthetic learning, 24–26
tactile perception and discrimination. *See also* kinesthetic-tactile learning
   activities and games for, 44, 58, 60, 69–70, 77–80, 93, 101–102
   for former print readers, 69–70
   symbol recognition, 41–42, 45–46, 59–61, 70, 83, 92
   teaching, 41–44
   two-handed reading approach, 42–44
   worksheets for developing, 101-102
tactual reading, 7–9. *See also* braille reading

both hands used, 9 (*see also* two-handed reading approach)
dominant and subordinate characters, 9
good *vs.* poor, 9
pauses and movements, 8
perception, 8
return sweeps and between-line movements, 9
taste sense development, 28–29
teaching braille reading. *See also* braille reading
   activities and games for (*see* activities and games)
   attitude and motivation development and, 35, 68–70
   audience for book on, 1
   braille code and, 1–2, 6–7, 47
   carryover skill development with, 52–55
   common approaches to, 16–17
   comprehension skill development with, 48–50, 65–68, 94, 99–100
   curriculum for, 17–18
   decoding skill development with, 45–47 (*see also* phonetic analysis)
   ergonomics and, 45 (*see also* book handling and position; posture)
   flexibility skill development with, 50–51, 68
   to former print readers, 57, 68–70
   in general education setting, 1, 34–36, 52–55, 98
   general education teacher role in, 52–53
   kinesthetic skill development with, 44–45
   mechanical skill development with, 36–41, 59–60, 67, 69
   overview of, 4–5
   precision teaching, 42–44, 69
   preschool experiences and, 4, 21–31
   rapid reading techniques for, 15, 34–56
   reading methods and, 2–4
   reading rate improvement with, 15–16, 67–68, 71, 94–97
   reading style development with, 51–52
   remedial reading interventions for, 5, 57–71
   tactile perception and discrimination with, 41–44, 69–70, 78–79, 81–92, 101–102
   teacher of students with visual impairments role in, 34–35, 52–53
   vocabulary development with, 47–48, 63–64, 82
technology innovations
   activities and games integrating, 97–98
   alternatives to braille and, 14–15
   braille reading and, 11–14, 15, 97–98
   sensory acuity and efficiency development, 26–27
ticktacktoe games, 96
tracking
   by former print readers, 70–71
   mechanical skill development, 36–41, 59–60, 67, 69
   reading rate and, 67, 70
   tactile perception and discrimination, 41–44
   visual, 21–22, 28
   warm-up, 70
transcription into braille
   courses in, 1–2
   for former print readers, 71
   in general education setting, 52–55
   object labels, 31, 35, 69, 80, 92–93
   sentence recognition and, 93–94

transcription into braille (*cont.*)
    technology innovations and, 13
    translation software for, 13
    UEB as standard for, 7
    vocabulary development and, 47–48
    word and phrase charts, 82–83
translation software, 13
treasure box game, 90
treasure house game, 91
Trouble game, 96
turn-about words, 50–51
two-handed reading approach, 7, 9, 10, 15–16, 38, 42–44

UEB Online, 2, 18
uncontracted braille, 10–11, 16, 42
Unified English Braille Australian Training Manual, 2
Unified English Braille Code (UEB), 6–7
Unified English Braille Transcription Course, 2

visual sense development, 27–28
vocabulary development, 47–48, 63–64, 82
Vowel Lotto, 63

warm-up tracking, 70
wheel of fortune game, 91–92
wiggle worm game, 85
word and phrase charts, 82–83
word families game, 92
Word PlayHouse, 60
word recognition game, 90
words category game, 91
words that start the same game, 90–91
wrist flexibility, activities for, 36

yes or no activity, 94